SONGS OF THE

T H E   D E C A D E   S E R I E S

14 Achy Breaky Heart (Don't Tell My Heart)

20 All for Love

25 All That She Wants

30 Always

38 Baby Baby

44 Beautiful in My Eyes

48 Beauty and the Beast

60 Can You Feel the Love Tonight

53 Colors of the Wind

68 Don't Know Much

80 End of the Road

84 Forever in Love

75 Forrest Gump - Main Title (Feather Theme)

88 Theme from "Frasier"

90 Friends in Low Places

94 Have I Told You Lately

98 Here and Now

104 Hero

110 Hold My Hand

126 How Am I Supposed to Live Without You

130 I Believe

138 I Don't Have the Heart

117 I'd Do Anything for Love (But I Won't Do That)

142 I'll Make Love to You

146 In the Still of the Nite (I'll Remember)

156 Losing My Religion

162 One Sweet Day

151 Opposites Attract

166 The Power of Love

171 The River of Dreams

178 Save the Best for Last

188 Theme from "Schindler's List"

183 The Sign

190 Tears in Heaven

194 Vision of Love

201 When I Fall in Love

214 A Whole New World (Aladdin's Theme)

208 With One Look

221 You Must Love Me

- *Laptop Computers*

- *Pagers*

- *Dream Teams*

OPRAH WINFREY REMAINED QUEEN OF DAYTIME TV.

THE NINETIES

THE 90s

BY ELAINE SCHMIDT

Speeding headlong toward the twenty-first century, Americans of th 1990s will probably be remembered by history as harried technology addicts racing through daily life with pagers beeping, cell-phones ringing, and e-mail messages flying. Shopping by catalog, cooking by microwave, chatting with virtual friends in cybe space, counting fat grams, and squeezing workouts into busy schedules adults of the nineties live life at an ever-increasing pace.

Americans of the nineties are living longer and retiring earlier than ever before in th country's history; in 1994 they sent *Modern Maturity* to the #1 spot on magazine subscription charts. With the first of the much-touted Baby Boom generation hitting the age of fifty in 1995, the Boomers' babies, dubbed Generation X, continued their struggle to find an identity comparable to that of their parents. In fashion, a retro craze rendered a second generation of young people victims of seventies styles, while their parents relaxed into a "working-casual" mode of dress.

Like any of the previous nine decades of the twentieth century the nineties have come to be defined by a few key events an trends. Events likely to survive in the memory of future generations are the baseball strike that canceled a World Series, the horrific bombing of the Oklahoma City federal building, the inescapa O.J. Simpson trial, the mysterious Unabomber, and the AIDS epidem But the trends by which the decade will eventually be defined may be harder t identify. Perhaps the nineties will be remembered as the decade of superlatives. Superstores, Dream Teams, the enormous Mall of America, and the information superhighway al point to the ever-growing American obsession with the biggest and best. From the Wonderbra in t world of lingerie to the mutation of the television set into high-definition, big-screen, surround-sound home theater, no area of American life has seemed safe from the quest for grandeur.

Techno-gadgetry may dominate the perception that future generations have of 1990s America. Encumbered with computers, cordless phones, fax machines, modems, pagers, cellular phones, desktop computers, laptops, and computerized date and phone books, the country seems to be on a continual mission of acquisition. Loathe to be found with outdated equipment, Americans have filled their lives with the latest in kitchen gadgets, fashions, automobiles, hand-held remotes to control as much as possible, and a levy of fitness contraptions and videos.

The decade of corporate down-sizing, the nineties may also be remembered as the era of Americans working at home. Whether self-employed or "tele-commuters," millions of Americans began reporting to offices with backyard views.

Entertainment, long a major influence on American life and culture, has taken on new dimensions in the nineties. As twenty-four-hour cable news and sports channels search the world for stories to fill their broadcast days, the lines between news and entertainment become increasingly blurred. Print news has thrived in national news magazines like *Newsweek*, *Time*, and *U.S. News and World Report*, while the immediacy of television and radio news has taken a predictable, heavy toll on local newspapers. Struggling to bolster declining readerships, many papers have begun offering on-line subscriptions.

Entertainment and politics found themselves nearly indistinguishable during the 1992 presidential campaign. Bill Clinton, the first member of his Baby Boom generation to be elected president, could be found hitting the campaign trail with a saxophone in hand. Clinton, incumbent George Bush, and diminutive Texas billionaire Ross Perot, who sashayed in and out of the race representing supporters he referred to as "the volunteers," lapped up air time anywhere they found it, from late-night television to "Larry King Live." Vice President Dan Quayle squared off against a television sitcom when a story line on "Murphy Brown" gave the title character a child out of wedlock.

More and more new mothers began choosing careers over full-time motherhood, for both personal and financial reasons, placing young children in the hands of professional child-care providers.

Clinton won the 1992 election by a narrow margin, promising disenchanted voters that he would reinvent government. Two years later, the country voted for still more change, giving control of Congress to the Republican party for the first time in forty years. Entertainers such as Rush Limbaugh have exacerbated the political divisiveness of the country, finding national media platforms for expressing their political opinions while remaining safely outside the political process. Comedian Al Franken managed a retort with his book *Rush Limbaugh Is a Big Fat Idiot*.

The age of bigger and better has perhaps best been reflected in Hollywood, where studios scramble to find the next mega-hit. The reliable formula of an action film featuring a major star, which had served well in the past, began to fail early in the decade. Dismal responses to *Waterworld* and *Cliffhanger* shook Hollywood's confidence, while the offbeat *Forrest Gump* baffled the experts, hit the $300 million mark at the box office, and became something of a touchstone of pop culture. Hollywood's sense of direction and identity was deeply shaken.

And then there were children's movies. The biggest box office hit of 1995 was Disney's *The Lion King*, but the receipts were only the beginning of the story. Like many other successful family films, it hit additional pay dirt with action figures sold through fast-food chains, books, cartoons, comic books, coloring books, lines of children's clothing and accessories,

dishes, sheets, towels, videos, video games, and recordings. Elton John wrote the music for the movie's songs and rode the wave of popularity with his recording of "Can You Feel the Love Tonight."

There would appear to be no discernible pattern to Hollywood's successful adult films. Nineties audiences have feasted on Jane Austen's *Sense and Sensibility*, wept over Steven Spielberg's *Schindler's List*, and embraced revisionist history through *Dances with Wolves*. The film industry continues to analyze the appetites of a movie-going public that would spend over $500 million on *The Lion King*, *Forrest Gump*, *True Lies*, *The Flintstones*, *Clear and Present Danger*, and *Interview with the Vampire* in the same year.

...EG RYAN BECAME A SILVER SCREEN DARLING.

Once upon a time, Hollywood looked to successful Broadway shows for movie ideas. Enter the nineties, and a painfully cautious Broadway began looking to Hollywood films for show ideas, hoping that success in one venue would ensure the same in another. If Hollywood is nervously seeking mega-hits, Broadway is doing so frantically. For a Broadway show to make money, it must run for several years; it costs a fortune to mount a Broadway spectacle. Producers and backers, justifiably terrified of financial disaster, are unwilling to risk money on anything that doesn't seem to offer sure success. This financially ultra-conservative Broadway of the nineties has seen revivals of *Show Boat*, *Carousel*, *Guys and Dolls*, and *How to Succeed in Business without Really Trying*. In the arena of new shows, Andrew Lloyd Webber, who has a long list of hits to his credit, has been one of the few bankable names; his *Sunset Boulevard* ("With One Look") is one of the most prominent shows of the decade.

has "Frasier," the witty, urbane "Cheers" spin-off.

Oh, yes, did we forget talk shows? We tried, but no one who owned a television in the nineties will ever forget the astonishing parade of truly disturbed and merely misfit individuals who've found their fifteen minutes of fame on the decade's countless talk shows. What Phil began and Oprah continued, Geraldo twisted. By mid nineties, Ricki Lake and a hefty roster of former child stars were putting nearly anything that breathed on the air, hoping for sensational outbursts and bizarre stories. The amazing thing is that people keep watching.

The publishing industry has also spent the decade reaching for the proverbial brass ring. Writers wishing to publish literary fiction have gotten a "Don't call us..." response from most publishers, while O.J., his attorneys and jurors, and nearly anyone who has ever laid eyes on the British royal family have instantly been extended the red carpet. Nonfiction has dominated the book market, from cook books to software manuals and *The Idiot's Guide to...* (insert virtually anything here).

DR. FRASIER CRANE, A FAMILIAR TV CHARACTER IN THE 1980S ON "CHEERS," WENT ON TO HAVE HIS OWN HIT SITCOM IN THE 1990S.

"If it works—copy it," seems to be the credo of nineties television execs thus far. "Roseanne" worked—enter "Grace Under Fire." "Seinfeld" worked—let's bring on "Friends," "Mad About You," "Boston Common," and an entire pack of chummy urban sitcoms. "Beverly Hills 90210" begat "Melrose Place," which then begat a chic parade of upscale prime-time soaps. The animated "Simpsons" has defied copying, perhaps mercifully, as

Bookstores have undergone striking, swift changes. In 1990 a book-seeker would likely have headed for a local book shop, or the nearby mall, for a quick look around and simple book purchase. By mid decade the book superstore had descended upon most American cities, and an errand to purchase a book has suddenly become an adventure in browsing through recordings, newspapers of the local, national, or international varieties, software, stationery, greeting cards,

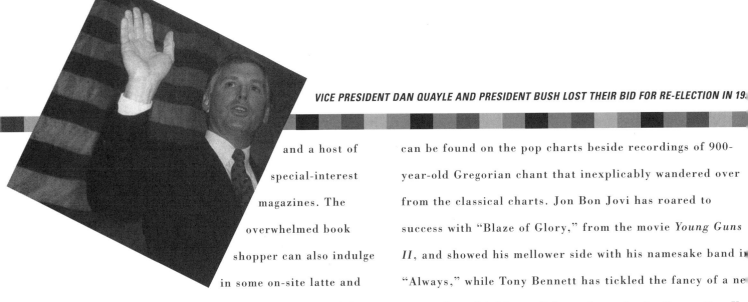

and a host of special-interest magazines. The overwhelmed book shopper can also indulge in some on-site latte and biscotti, or perhaps curl up in an overstuffed chair while perusing a possible selection.

There was a time when it was easy to define styles within the realm of popular music. People's tastes were fairly predictable by age and race. Not so in the nineties, where rap, the music of black urban youth, has had its biggest sales among white suburban teens, while country superstars have found their biggest audiences in large urban centers. The biggest trend in pop music of the nineties is the lack of a trend. Turn the radio dial, if you can still find a radio with a dial, and you are likely to find alternative rock, hip-hop, classic rock, light jazz, country, folk, and grunge on the airwaves. Radio stations no longer play the same Top 40 records from coast to coast.

LAPTOP COMPUTERS BECAME AN ICON OF THE ERA.

No one is sure where to look for a hit, or whom to target as consumers. The industry appears to be taking a shotgun approach. The result of this confusion is a growing banquet of choices available to the listener. People look for what they want to hear and take it with them via personal CD players, car stereos, and the like.

This individual freedom in pop music has meant that the striking, stylized sounds of Mariah Carey ("Hero," "Vision of Love"), Luther Vandross ("Here and Now"), and Boyz II Men ("End of the Road," "In the Still of the Nite")

can be found on the pop charts beside recordings of 900-year-old Gregorian chant that inexplicably wandered over from the classical charts. Jon Bon Jovi has roared to success with "Blaze of Glory," from the movie *Young Guns II*, and showed his mellower side with his namesake band in "Always," while Tony Bennett has tickled the fancy of a new generation with his renditions of standards. Generation X-ers, feeling disenfranchised by society in general and by pop music in particular, have turned to the folk-rock sounds of former frat band Hootie and the Blowfish, putting "Hold My Hand" onto the charts. Ace of Base ("The Sign," "All That She Wants") has also benefited from this Gen-X attention, as have initial-bands R.E.M. ("Losing My Religion") and EMF ("I Believe").

The superstar trend has brought crossover fame to a new breed of country musicians. Garth Brooks scored a huge hit with "Friends Low Places" and has sold tens of millions of albums. For a while, Billy Ray Cyrus's "Achy Breaky Heart" was *everywhere*. Still, country music die-hards have mourned the disappearance of stars of the Waylon Jennings and Willie Nelson ilk. Superstars of another stripe have emerged from an unexpected quarter: "The Three Tenors"—classical singers Jose Carreras, Placido Domingo, and Luciano Pavarotti—have garnered huge successes in recordings, videos, concerts, and books, touring the world and keeping classical music alive before throngs of adoring fans. Their first album together sold twelve million copies worldwide.

Duets have enjoyed a resurgence in popularity, perhaps led by Frank Sinatra's collaborations with a variety of pop music's hot properties. Celine Dion teamed with Clive Griffin to resurrect the standard "When I Fall In Love" for the movie *Sleepless in Seattle*, and joined Peabo Bryson to record the title track for Disney's *Beauty and the Beast*. Bryson changed partners for the follow-up hit, singing "A Whole New World" from *Aladdin*, with Regina Belle. Linda Ronstadt and Aaron Neville blended voices for the tender "Don't Know Much." Meanwhile, another partnership upped the ante: Bryan Adams, Rod Stewart, and Sting were a trio in "All for Love," the theme song for—what else?—*The Three Musketeers*.

With the golden age of rock now a part of history, audiences have rushed to hear reunion tours of bands like the Eagles. Boxed sets featuring the complete or "best-of" recordings of now-defunct bands or singers sell like hot cakes while bestowing classic status on the artists. Even The Beatles made a comeback in 1995 and '96, via "a new release," anthology albums, and an extended television documentary.

Baby Boomers have held on to their favorite pop stars as younger audiences have discovered them, extending the careers of the now-middle-aged artists to multiple decades. Eric Clapton started an "unplugged"

CAL RIPKEN, JR. BECAME A SPORTS LEGEND BY BREAKING LOU GEHRIG'S MAJOR LEAGUE RECORD OF CONSECUTIVE GAMES PLAYED.

trend with his 1992 album of the same name, rearranging the 1971 hit "Layla" and including the wrenching "Tears in Heaven," about the death of his young son. Rod Stewart and Van Morrison both charted with Morrison's "Have I Told You Lately." Elton John, in addition to racking up hits with Disney, provided a blast from the past by redoing his 1974 single "Don't Let the Sun Go Down on Me" with George Michael. Meat Loaf staged a revival of his one-album career with "I'd Do Anything for Love (But I Won't Do That)." Billy Joel tried to cross "The River of Dreams," but not before reminding fans and junior-high history teachers alike that "We Didn't Start the Fire."

EAKER OF THE HOUSE NEWT GINGRICH LED THE REPUBLICAN MAJORITY HOUSE ELECTED IN 1994.

For those of us muddling our way through our daily lives in the waning years of the twentieth century, weighty events seem to resound, drowning out what is lighthearted, frivolous, and fun. We look at globalization and the World Wide Web and wonder if humankind is pulling together. We look at NAFTA and the European Community and fear that perhaps we are all circling our wagons. We see the disarray in the former Soviet Union and wonder how long it will be before our own alliances fail. We keep a watchful eye to the pressure cooker that is the Middle East, as we wonder who on the planet will acquire nuclear arms next. At home we are inundated with statistics from a media industry determined to wrap up the slightest American economic, demographic, or entertainment twitch as a trend, and we stave off retail bombardment at every turn. We fret about being victims of violent crime, outfitting our homes, cars, computers, and even our persons with security devices. Yet we have social and career freedoms that would have been unthinkable as recently as the middle of the century. We are beginning to learn to use technology rather than be enslaved by it, and we are a healthier people than the world has ever seen. If we look ahead to the next century with a wary eye, perhaps it is simply a reflection of the tumultuous century we are exiting. Life has changed radically in the past century, with the most dramatic changes occurring since World War II. Whether they be the best or the worst of times, they are our times, and the diversity and personal freedom they offer are unique in the history of the world.

THE NINETIES

STATISTICS

CADEMY AWARDS – BEST FILM

1990 - *DANCES WITH WOLVES*

1991 - *THE SILENCE OF THE LAMBS*

1992 - *UNFORGIVEN*

1993 - *SCHINDLER'S LIST*

1994 - *FORREST GUMP*

1995 - *BRAVEHEART*

ORLD SERIES

1990 - CINCINNATI OVER OAKLAND

1991 - MINNESOTA OVER ATLANTA

1992 - TORONTO OVER ATLANTA

1993 - TORONTO OVER PHILADELPHIA

1994 - WORLD SERIES CANCELED DUE TO PLAYERS' STRIKE

1995 - ATLANTA OVER CLEVELAND

STATISTICS

1989–1990 SEASON

OUTSTANDING DRAMA SERIES: "L.A. LAW"

OUTSTANDING COMEDY SERIES: "MURPHY BROWN"

1990–1991 SEASON

OUTSTANDING DRAMA SERIES: "L.A. LAW"

OUTSTANDING COMEDY SERIES: "CHEERS"

1991–1992 SEASON

OUTSTANDING DRAMA SERIES: "NORTHERN EXPOSURE"

OUTSTANDING COMEDY SERIES: "MURPHY BROWN"

1992–1993 SEASON

OUTSTANDING DRAMA SERIES: "PICKET FENCES"

OUTSTANDING COMEDY SERIES: "SEINFELD"

1993–1994 SEASON

OUTSTANDING DRAMA SERIES: "PICKET FENCES"

OUTSTANDING COMEDY SERIES: "FRASIER"

1994–1995 SEASON

OUTSTANDING DRAMA SERIES: "NYPD BLUE"

OUTSTANDING COMEDY SERIES: "FRASIER"

TOP TEN TV SHOWS (MOST-WATCHED)

1989–1990

1. "ROSEANNE"
2. "THE BILL COSBY SHOW"
3. "CHEERS"
4. "A DIFFERENT WORLD"
5. "AMERICA'S FUNNIEST HOME VIDEOS"
6. "THE GOLDEN GIRLS"
7. "60 MINUTES"
8. "THE WONDER YEARS"
9. "EMPTY NEST"
10. "CHICKEN SOUP"

1990–1991

1. "CHEERS"
2. "60 MINUTES"
3. "ROSEANNE"
4. "A DIFFERENT WORLD"
5. "THE BILL COSBY SHOW"
6. "NFL MONDAY NIGHT FOOTBALL"
7. "AMERICA'S FUNNIEST HOME VIDEOS"
8. "MURPHY BROWN"
9. "AMERICA'S FUNNIEST PEOPLE"
10. "DESIGNING WOMEN"

1. "60 Minutes"

2. "Roseanne"

3. "Murphy Brown"

4. "Cheers"

5. "Home Improvement"

6. "Designing Women"

7. "Coach"

8. "Full House"

9. "Murder, She Wrote"

10. "Unsolved Mysteries"

1. "60 Minutes"

2. "Roseanne"

3. "Home Improvement"

4. "Murphy Brown"

5. "Murder, She Wrote"

6. "Coach"

7. "NFL Monday Night Football"

8. "The CBS Sunday Night Movie"

9. "Cheers"

10. "Full House"

1. "Home Improvement"

2. "60 Minutes"

3. "Seinfeld"

4. "Roseanne"

5. "Ellen"

6. "Grace Under Fire"

7. "Frasier"

8. "Coach"

9. "Murder, She Wrote"

10. "NFL Monday Night Football"

1. "Seinfeld"

2. "E.R."

3. "Home Improvement"

4. "Grace Under Fire"

5. "NFL Monday Night Football"

6. "60 Minutes"

7. "NYPD Blue"

8. "Friends"

9. "Roseanne"

10. "Murder, She Wrote" (tied with No. 9)

THE NINETIES

ACHY BREAKY HEART
(Don't Tell My Heart)

Words and Music by
DON VON TRESS

You can tell the world you nev - er was my girl.____
You can tell your ma I moved to Ark - an - sas.____

You can burn my clothes when I'm gone. Or you can tell your friends_ just
You can tell your dog to bite my leg. Or tell your broth - er Cliff__ whose

15

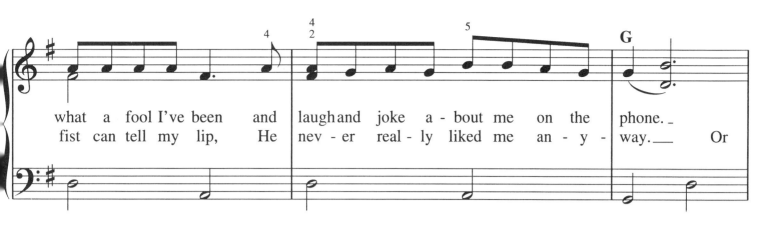

what a fool I've been and laugh and joke a-bout me on the phone.
fist can tell my lip, He nev-er real-ly liked me an-y-way. Or

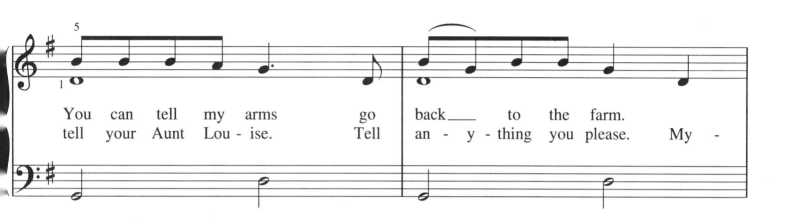

You can tell my arms go back to the farm.
tell your Aunt Lou-ise. Tell an-y-thing you please. My -

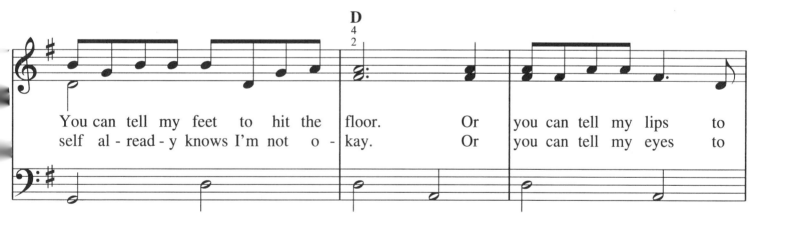

You can tell my feet to hit the floor. Or you can tell my lips to
self al-read-y knows I'm not o-kay. Or you can tell my eyes to

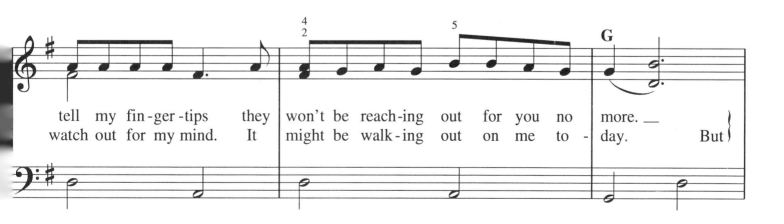

tell my fin-ger-tips they won't be reach-ing out for you no more.
watch out for my mind. It might be walk-ing out on me to-day. But

16

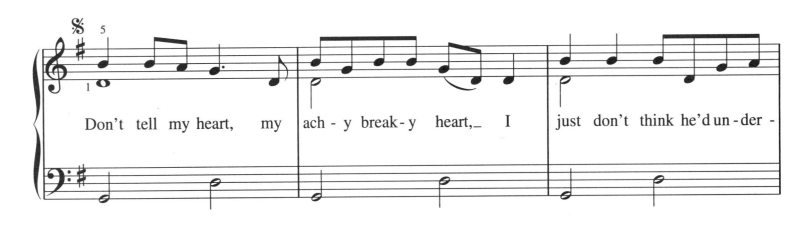

Don't tell my heart, my ach-y break-y heart,— I just don't think he'd un-der-

stand. And if you tell my heart, my ach-y break-y heart,— he

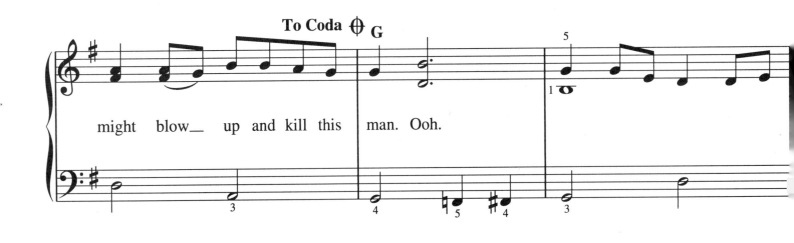

might blow— up and kill this man. Ooh.

D.S. al Coda

CODA

man.

Don't tell my heart, my

ach - y break - y heart, _ I

just don't think he'd un - der - stand. And

18

if you tell my heart, my ach - y break - y heart, __ he

might blow __ up and kill this man. Ooh.

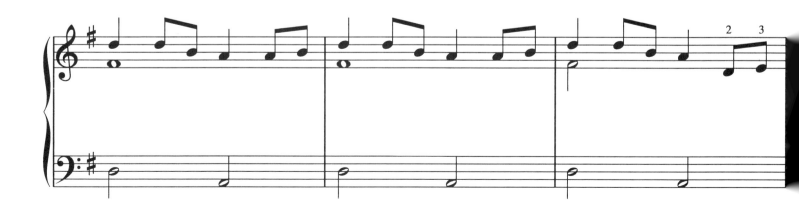

ALL FOR LOVE

(From Walt Disney Pictures' "THE THREE MUSKETEERS")

Words and Music by BRYAN ADAMS,
ROBERT JOHN "MUTT" LANGE and MICHAEL KAMEN

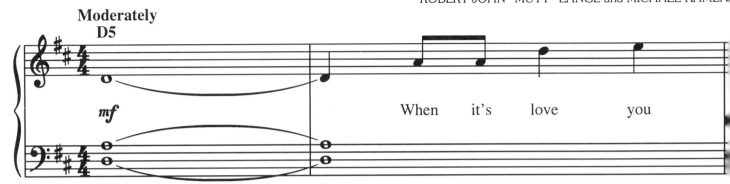

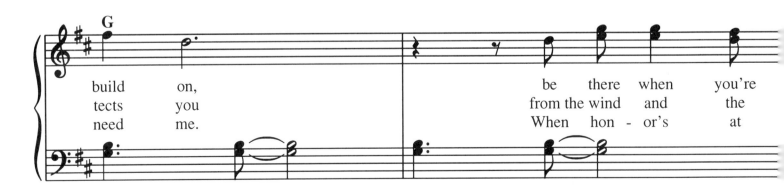

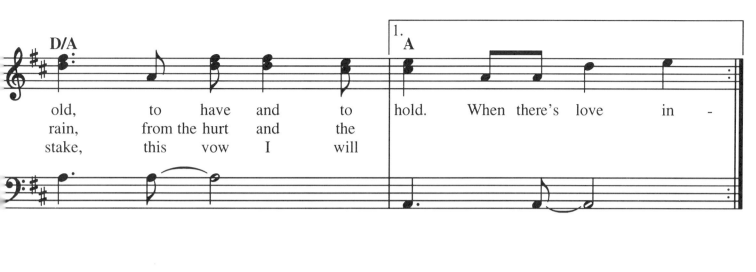

old, to have and to hold. When there's love in -
rain, from the hurt and to the
stake, this vow I will

pain.
make: Let's make it / that it's } all for one and all for

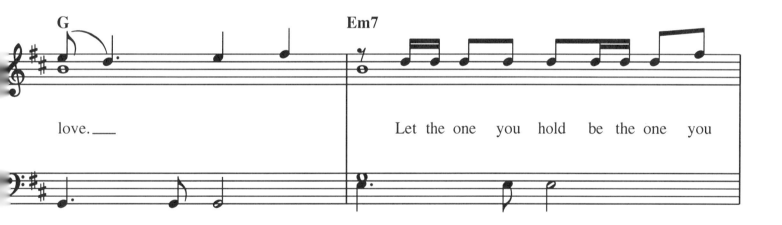

love.___ Let the one you hold be the one you

want, the one you need, 'cause when it's all for one it's one for

22

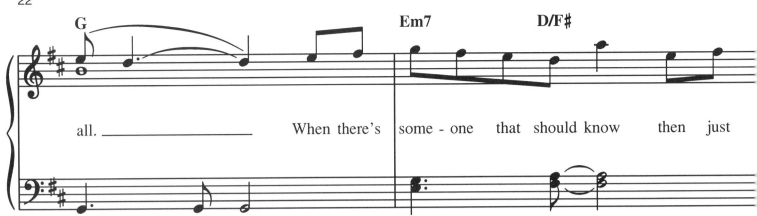

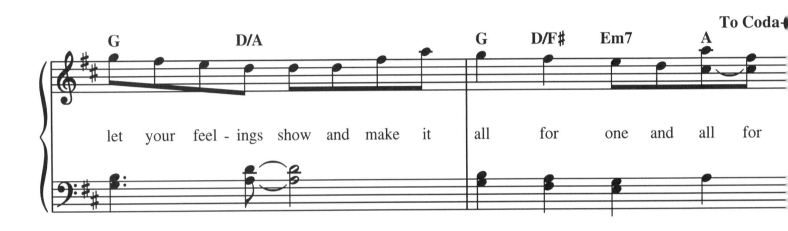

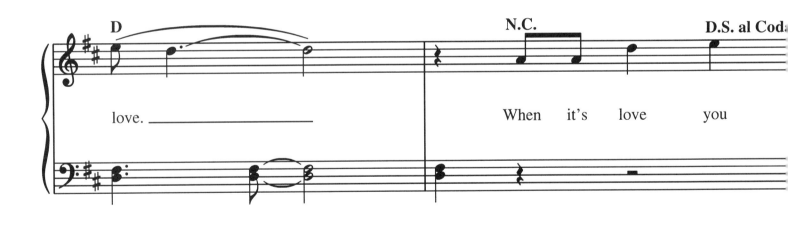

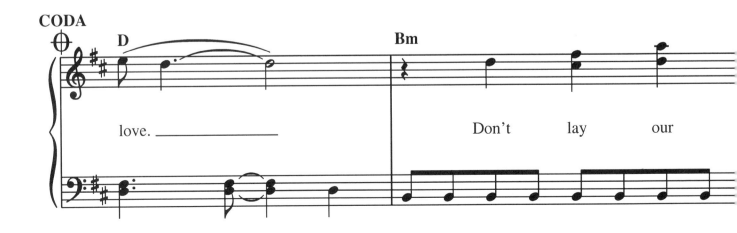

24

ALL THAT SHE WANTS

Words and Music by buddha, joker,
jenny and linn

Reggae pop beat

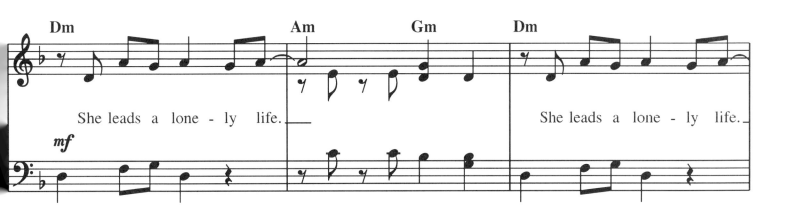

She leads a lone - ly life. ___ She leads a lone - ly life. ___

Well she woke up late in the morn - ing light and the

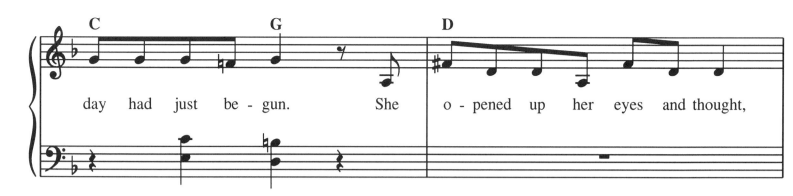

day had just be - gun. She o - pened up her eyes and thought,

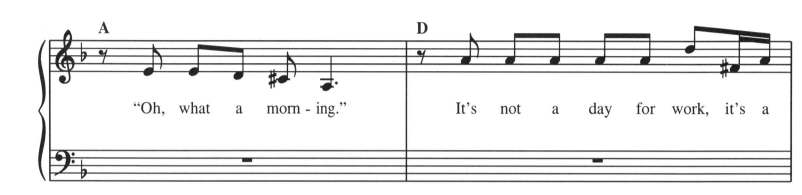

"Oh, what a morn - ing." It's not a day for work, it's a

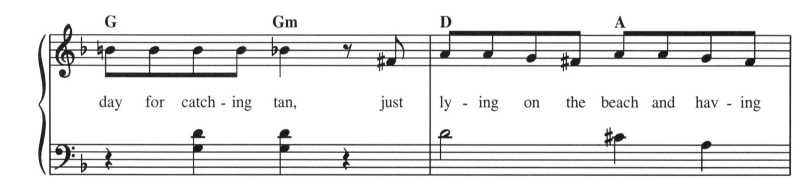

day for catch - ing tan, just ly - ing on the beach and hav - ing

fun. She's going to get __ ya. All __ that she wants is __ an - oth - er

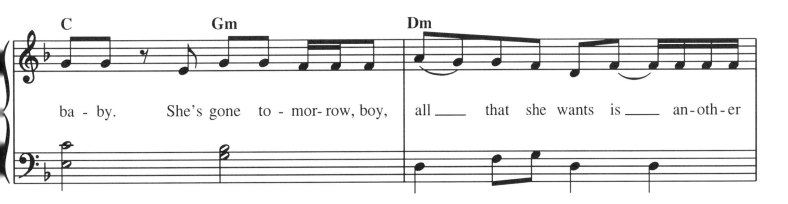

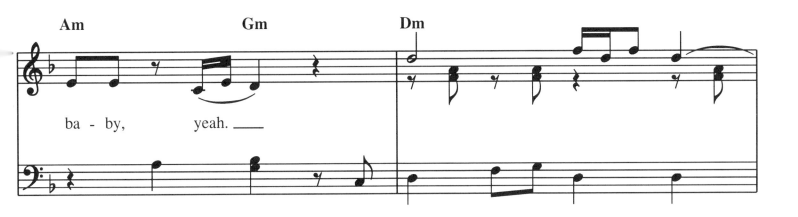

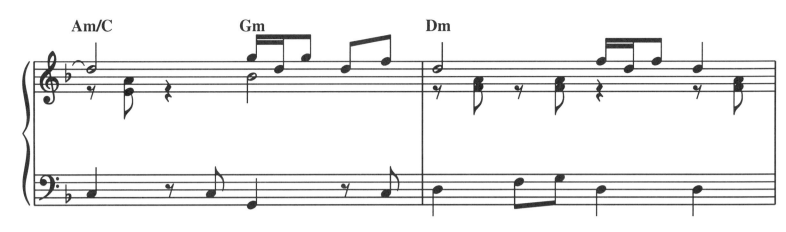

All that she wants. So if you

are in - side and the day is right, she's the hun - ter, you're the fox. A

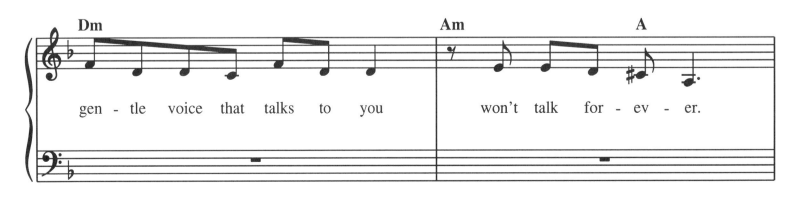

gen - tle voice that talks to you won't talk for - ev - er.

It is a night for pas - sion where the morn - ing means good - bye. Be -

ware of what is flash - ing in her eyes. She's going to get __ ya.

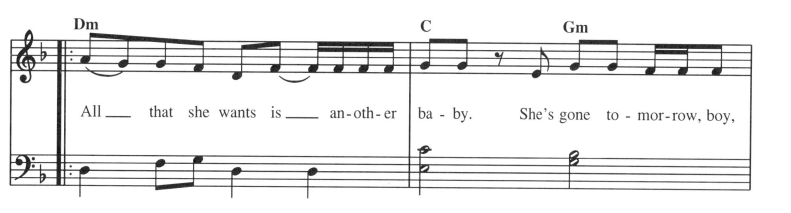

All __ that she wants is __ an - oth - er ba - by. She's gone to - mor - row, boy,

Repeat ad lib.

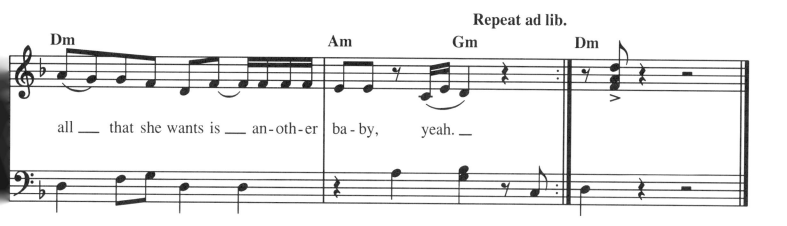

all __ that she wants is __ an - oth - er ba - by, yeah. __

ALWAYS

Words and Music by
JON BON JOVI

Slow rock ballad

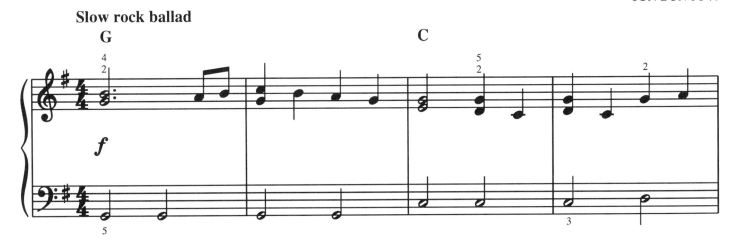

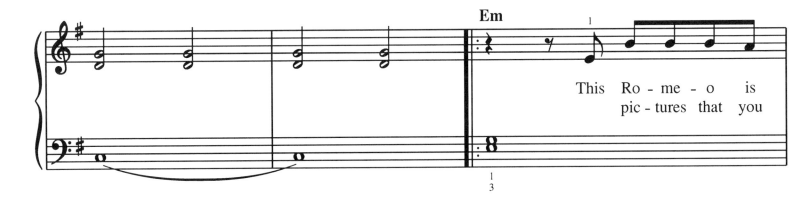

This Ro - me - o is
pic - tures that you

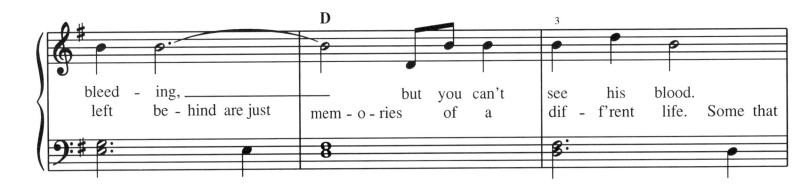

bleed - ing, _____ but you can't see his blood.
left be - hind are just mem - o - ries of a dif - f'rent life. Some that

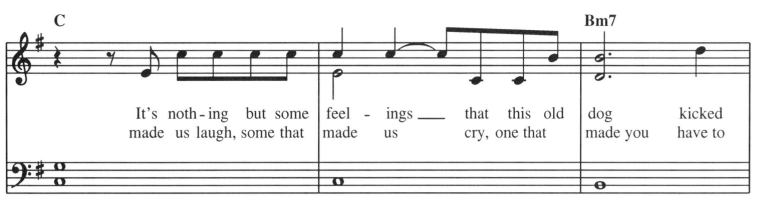

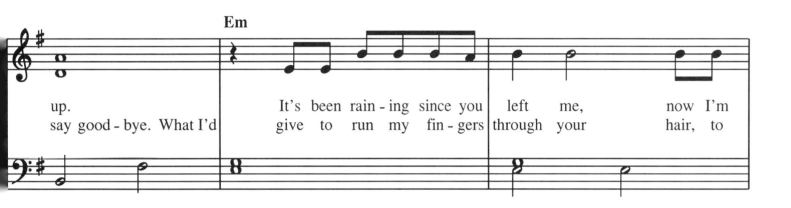

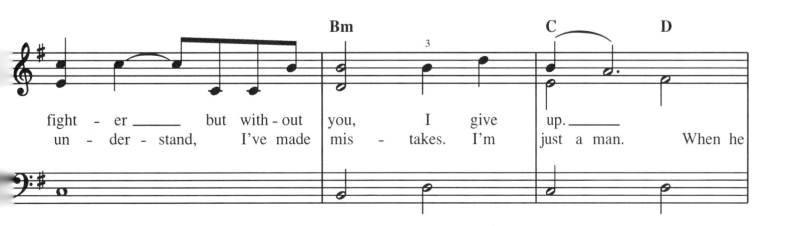

Now I can't sing a love song like the way it's meant to
holds you close, when he pulls you near, when he says the words you've been

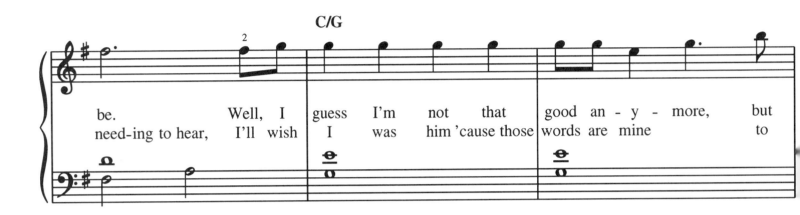

be. Well, I guess I'm not that good an - y - more, but
need-ing to hear, I'll wish I was him 'cause those words are mine to

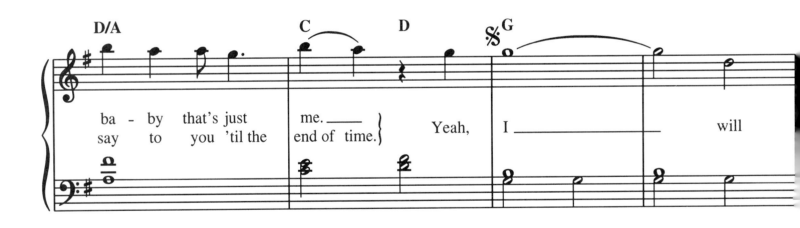

ba - by that's just me. Yeah, I will
say to you 'til the end of time.

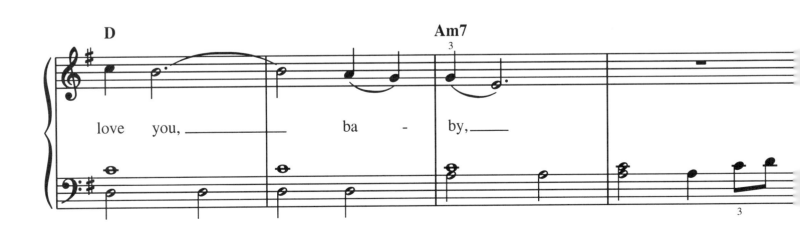

love you, ba - by,

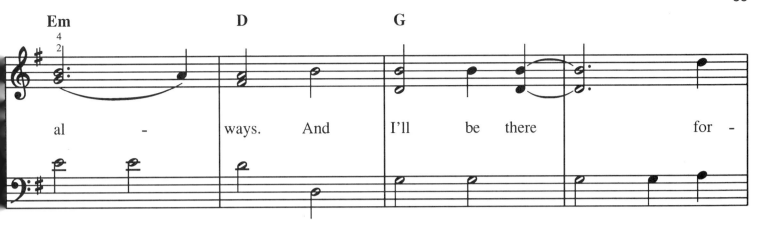

al - ways. And I'll be there for -

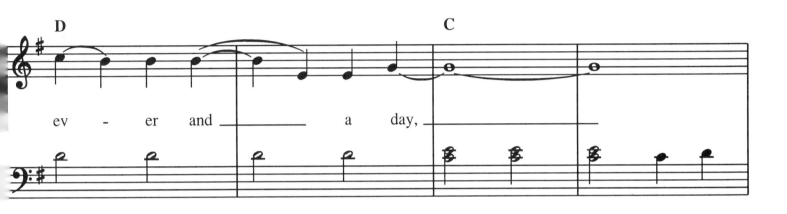

ev - er and ____ a day, ____

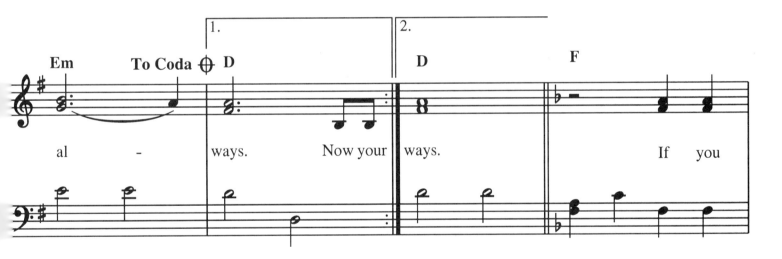

al - ways. Now your ways. If you

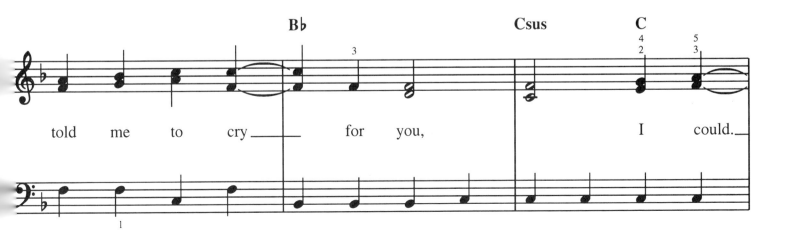

told me to cry ____ for you, I could. __

34

If you told me to die ____ for you ____

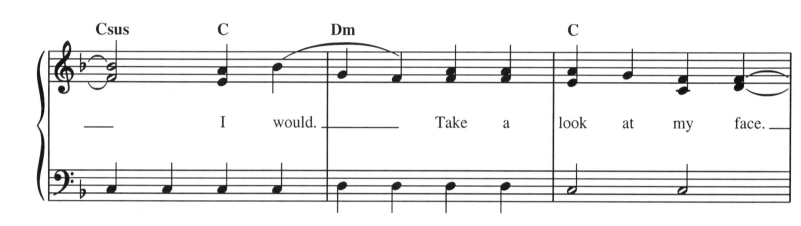

I would. ____ Take a look at my face. ____

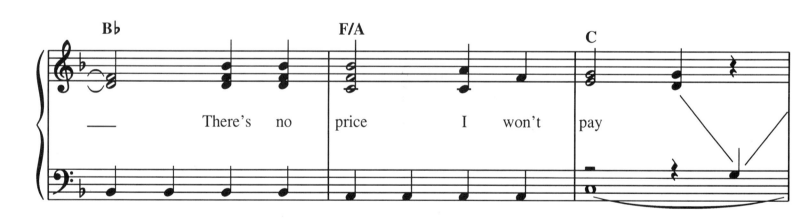

There's no price I won't pay

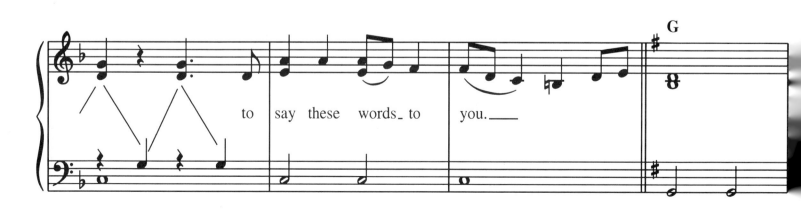

to say these words to you. ____

Well, there

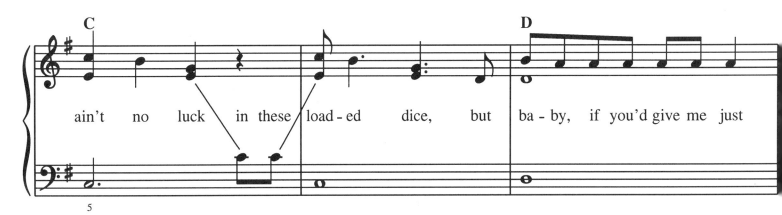

ain't   no   luck   in these / load-ed   dice,   but   ba-by,   if you'd give me just

one   more   try   we can   pack   up   our   old   dreams and   our   old   lives.   We'll

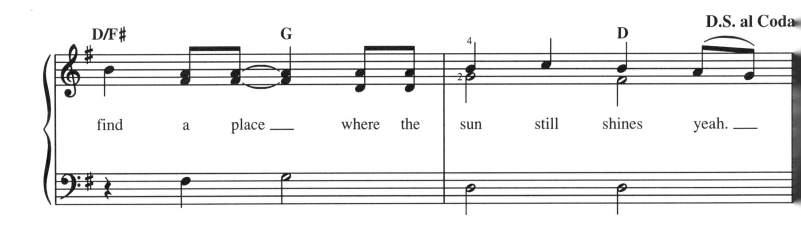

find   a   place ___   where the   sun   still   shines   yeah. ___

ways.   I'll   be   there   'til the   stars   don't   shine,   'til the

heav-ens burst and the words don't rhyme. I know when I die you'll be

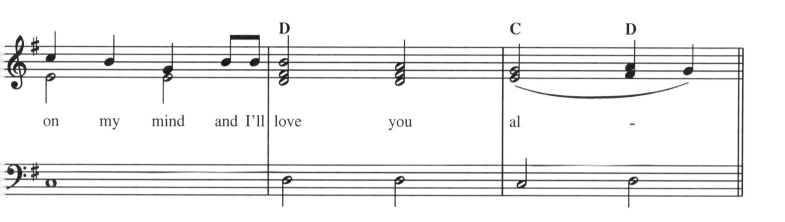

on my mind and I'll love you al -

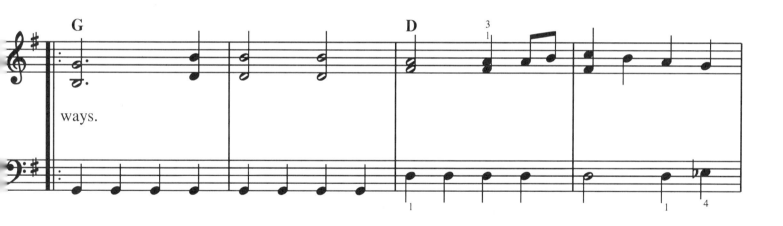

ways.

Repeat and Fade

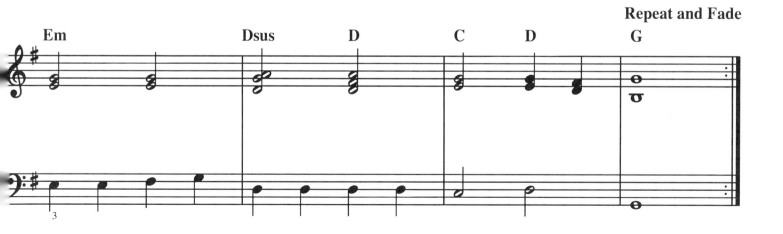

BABY BABY

Words and Music by AMY GRANT
and KEITH THOMAS

Moderately, not too fast

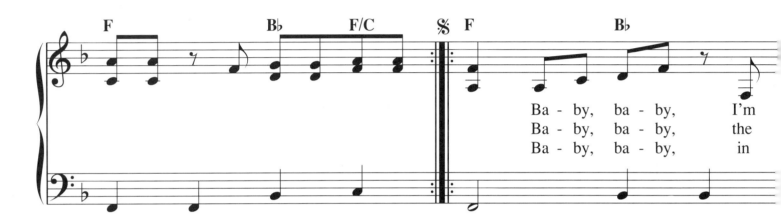

Ba - by, ba - by, I'm
Ba - by, ba - by, the
Ba - by, ba - by, in

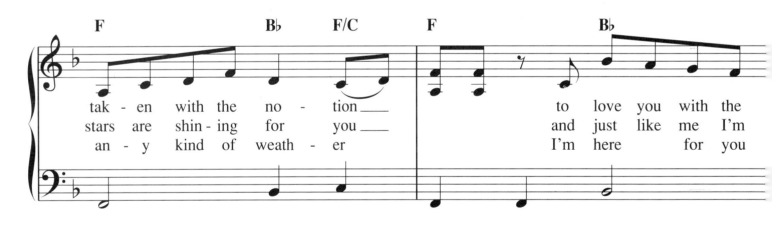

tak - en with the no - tion
stars are shin - ing for you
an - y kind of weath - er

to love you with the
and just like me I'm
I'm here for you

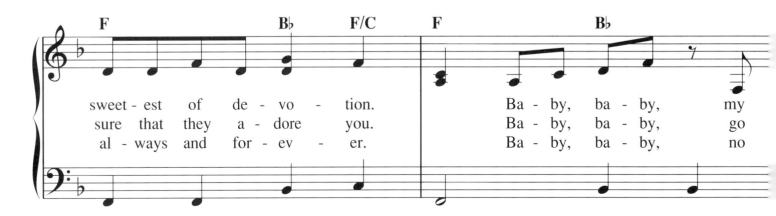

sweet - est of de - vo - tion.
sure that they a - dore you.
al - ways and for - ev - er.

Ba - by, ba - by, my
Ba - by, ba - by, go
Ba - by, ba - by, no

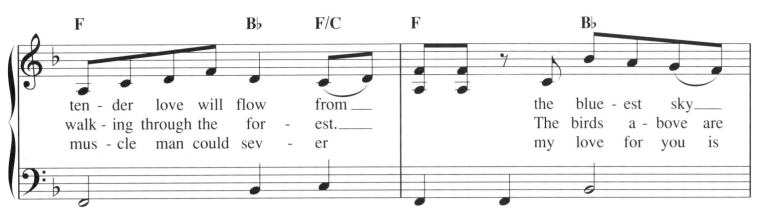

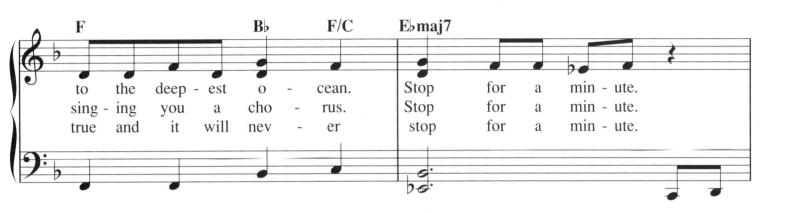

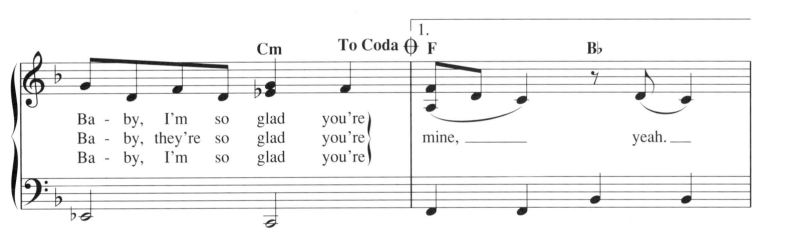

40

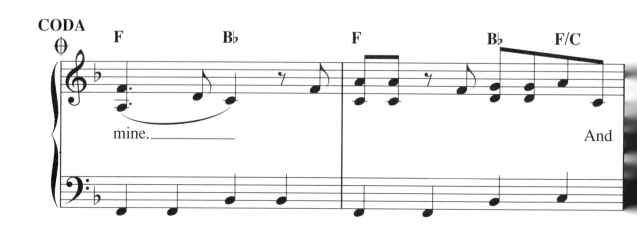

ev - er since the day you put my heart in mo - tion,

ba - by, I re - a - lize_____ there's no get - ting o - ver you.

42

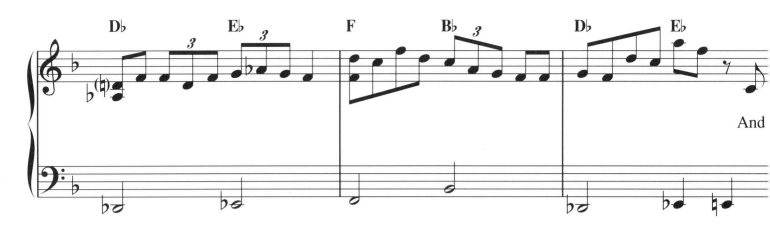

And

ev - er since the day you put my heart in mo - tion, ba - by, I re - al - ize that there's

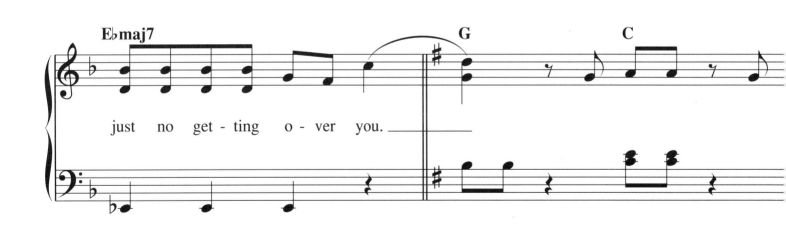

just no get - ting o - ver you.

o - ver you.

43

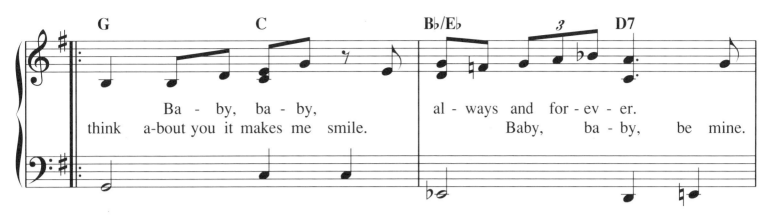

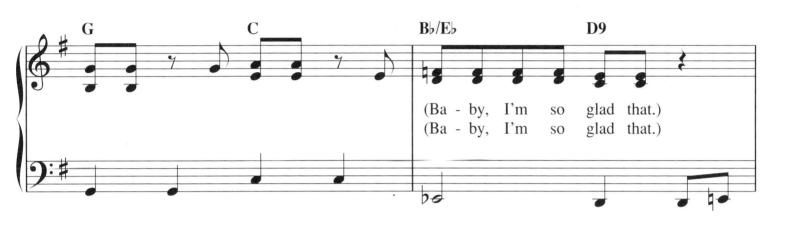

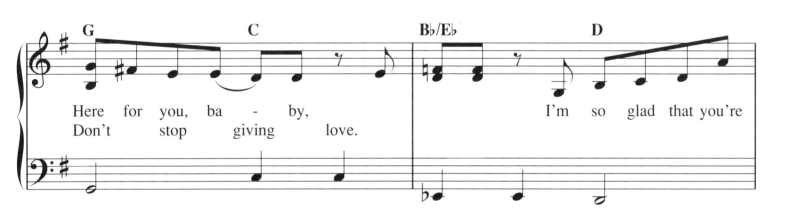

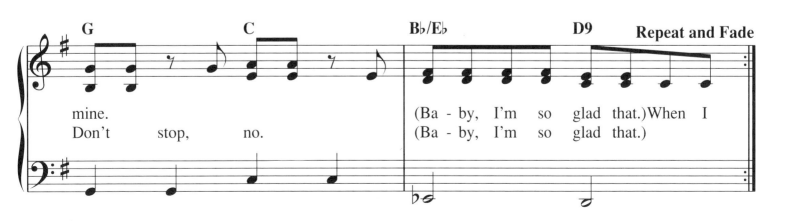

BEAUTIFUL IN MY EYES

Words and Music by
JOSHUA KADISON

46

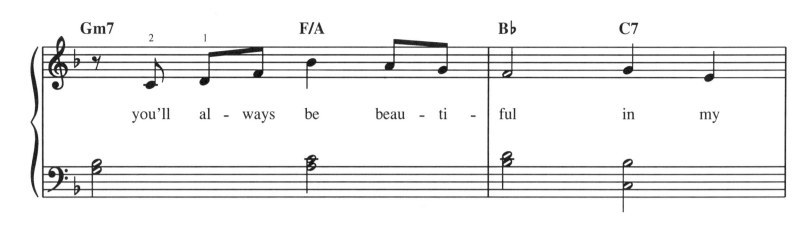

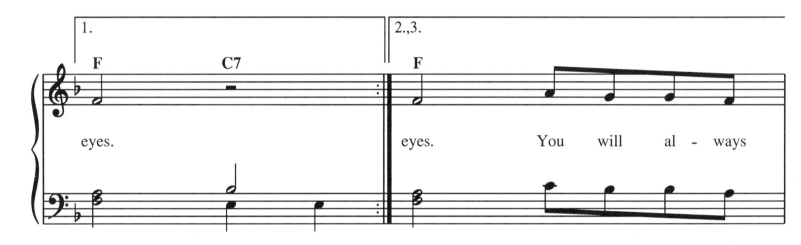

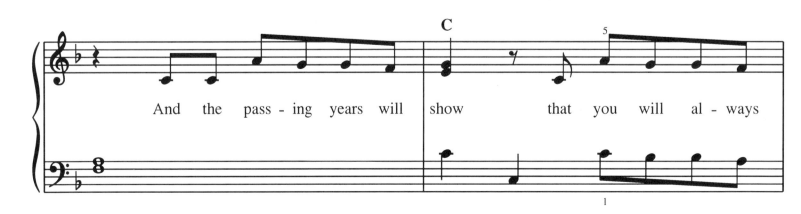

BEAUTY AND THE BEAST
from Walt Disney's BEAUTY AND THE BEAST

Lyrics by HOWARD ASHMAN
Music by ALAN MENKEN

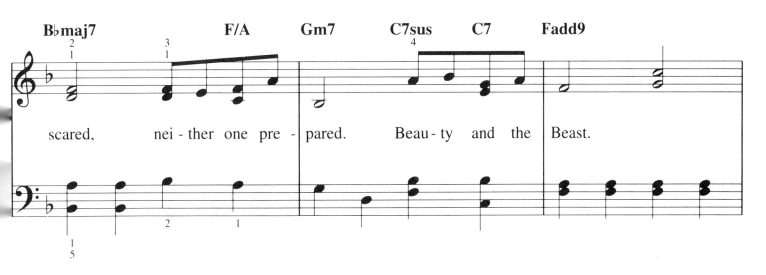

50

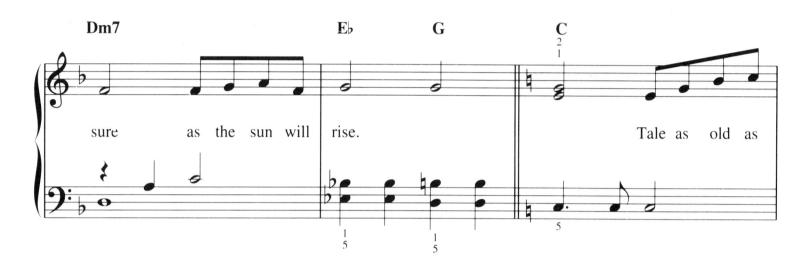

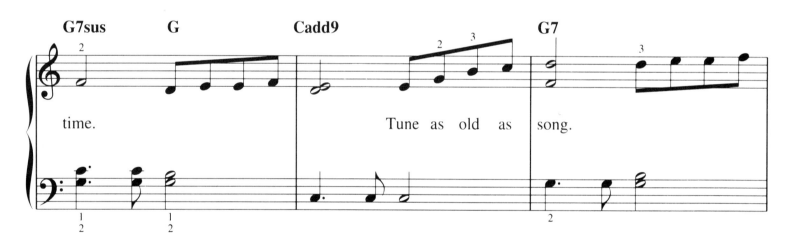

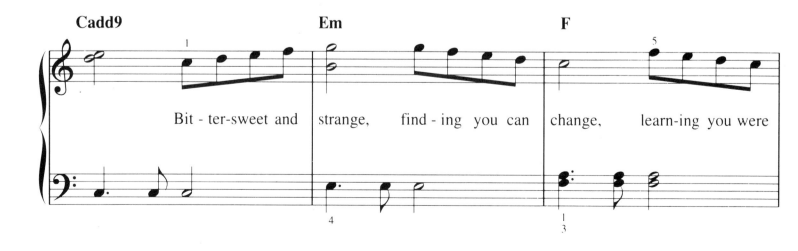

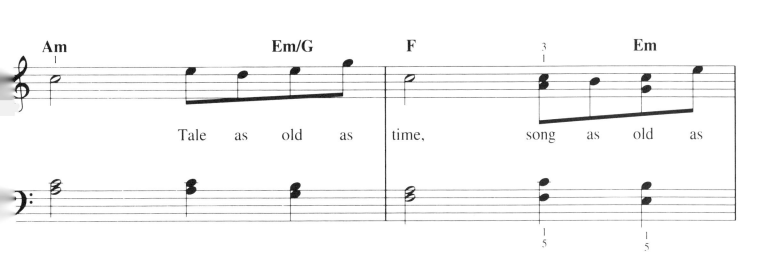

rhyme. Beau - ty and the Beast.

a tempo

COLORS OF THE WIND
from Walt Disney's POCAHONTAS

Music by ALAN MENKEN
Lyrics by STEPHEN SCHWARTZ

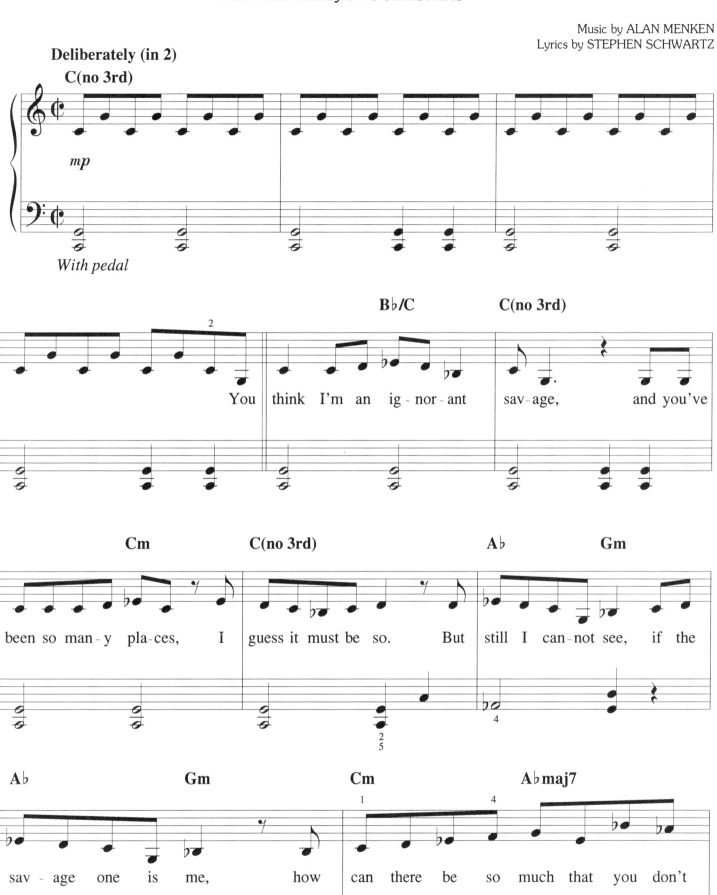

Moderately ♩ = ♩

G(no 3rd) N.C.   C   Am

know?   You don't   know...

mf

C   Am   C

rit.

You think you own what-ev - er land you

a tempo

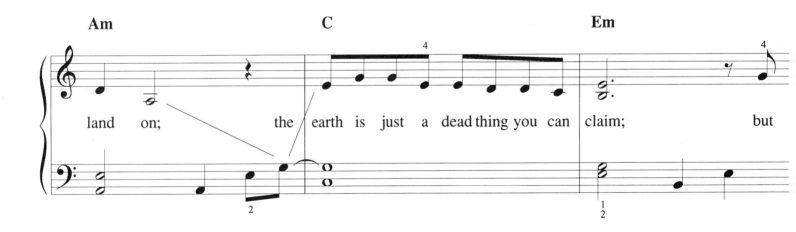

Am   C   Em

land on;   the earth is just a dead thing you can claim;   but

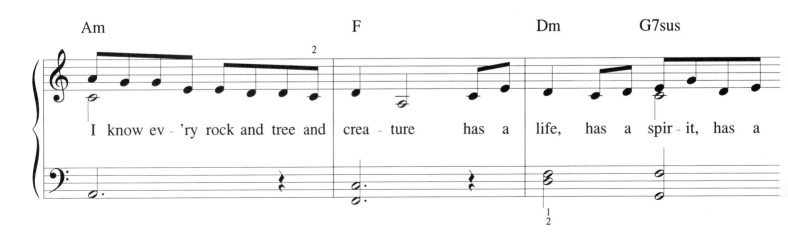

Am   F   Dm   G7sus

I know ev - 'ry rock and tree and crea - ture   has a   life, has a spir - it, has a

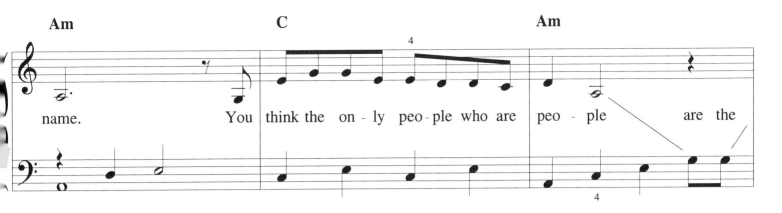

name. You think the on - ly peo - ple who are peo - ple are the

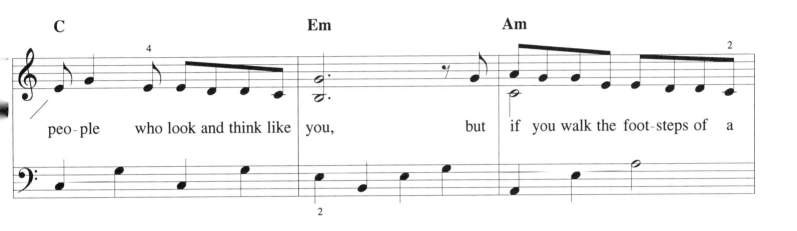

peo - ple who look and think like you, but if you walk the foot-steps of a

strang - er you'll learn things you nev - er knew you nev - er knew. Have you

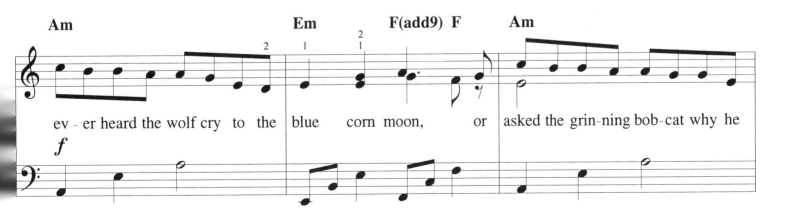

ev - er heard the wolf cry to the blue corn moon, or asked the grin-ning bob-cat why he

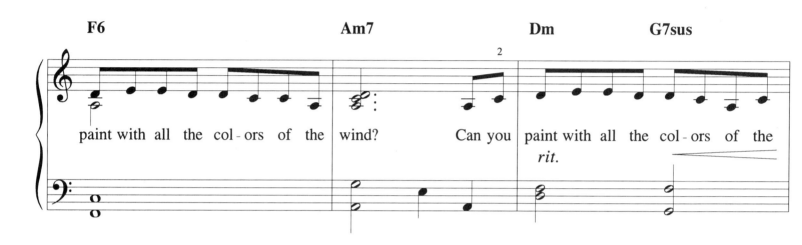

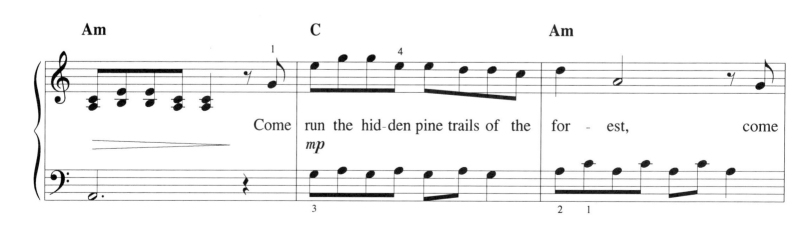

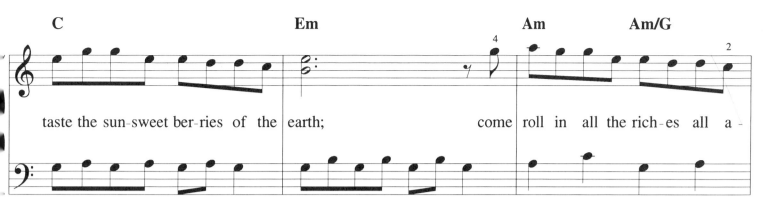

C   **Em**   **Am**   **Am/G**

taste the sun-sweet ber-ries of the earth;   come roll in all the rich-es all a -

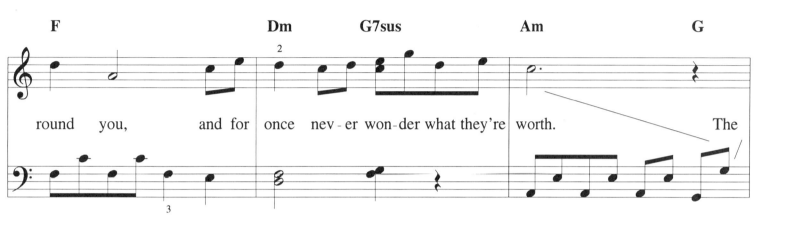

F   **Dm**   **G7sus**   **Am**   **G**

round you,   and for once nev-er won-der what they're worth.   The

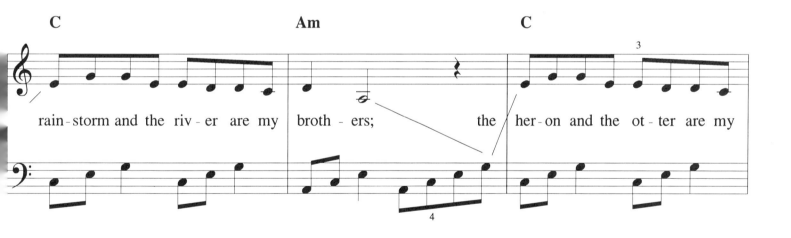

C   **Am**   **C**

rain-storm and the riv - er are my broth - ers;   the her-on and the ot-ter are my

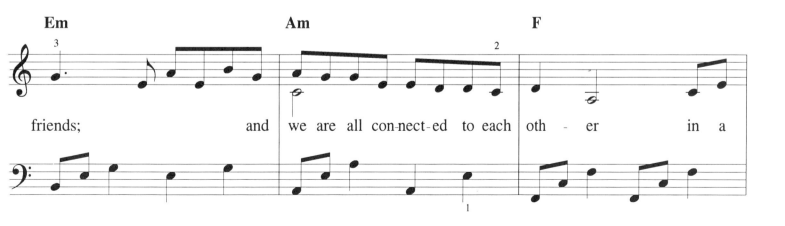

Em   **Am**   **F**

friends;   and we are all con-nect-ed to each oth - er   in a

58

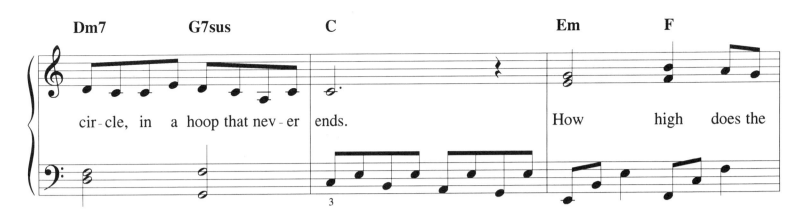

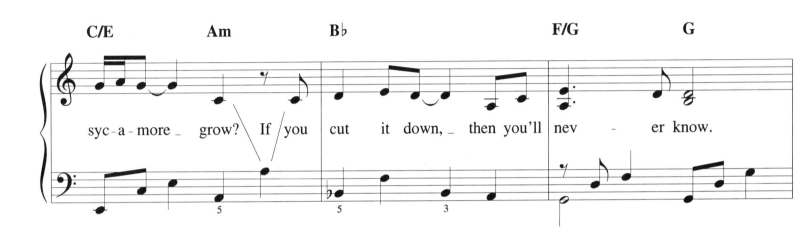

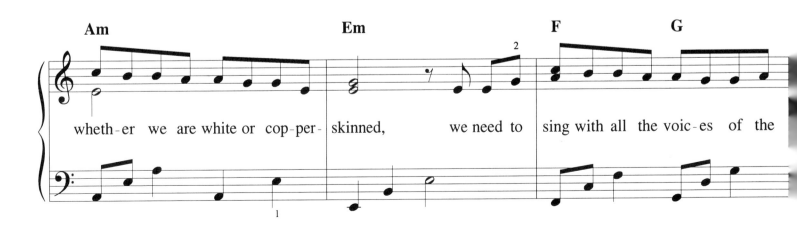

CAN YOU FEEL THE LOVE TONIGHT

Music by ELTON JOHN
Lyrics by TIM RICE

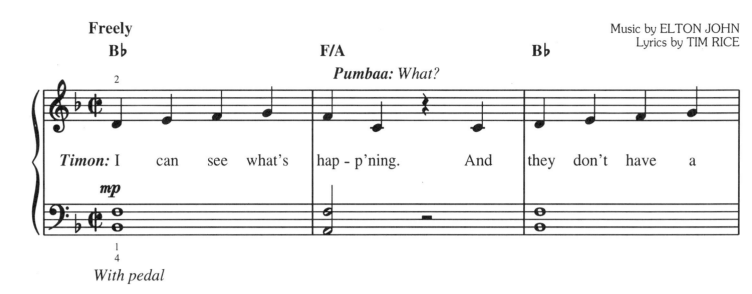

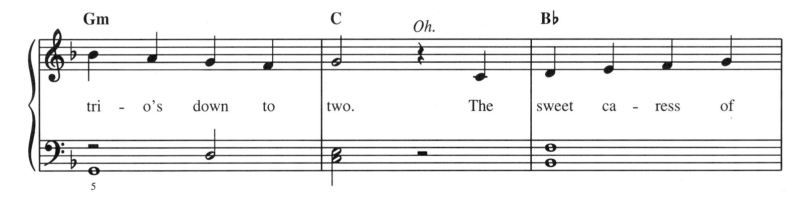

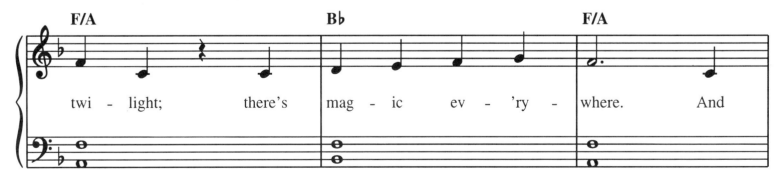

61

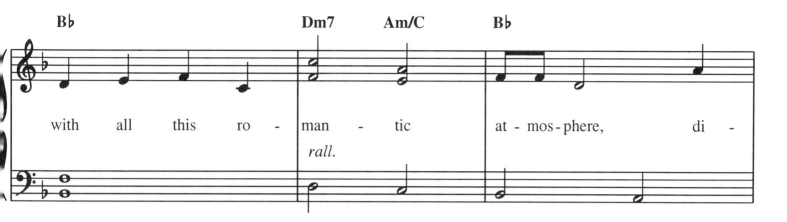

with all this ro - man - tic   at - mos - phere,   di -
rall.

Moderately (in two)

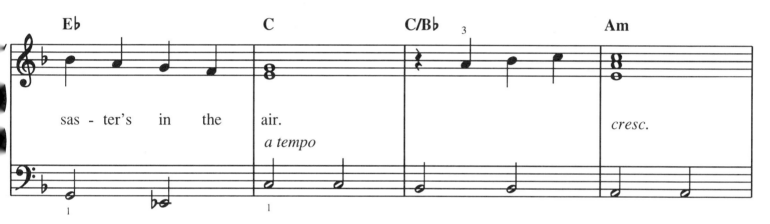

sas - ter's in the air.   *cresc.*
a tempo

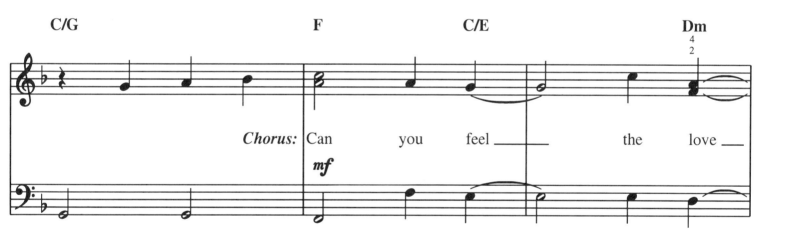

Chorus: Can   you   feel ___   the   love ___
mf

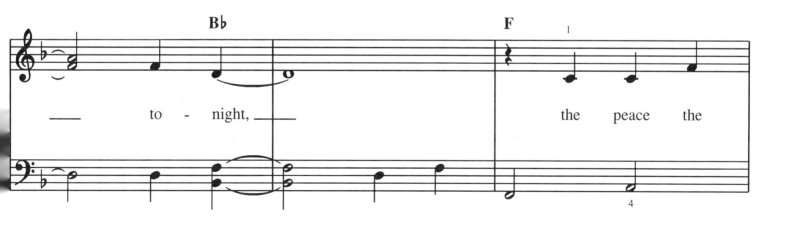

___ to - night, ___   the   peace   the

62

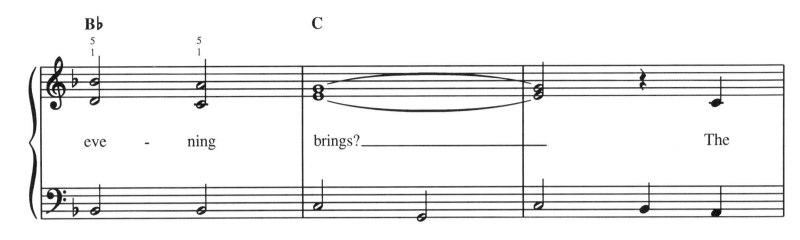

eve - ning   brings?_____   The

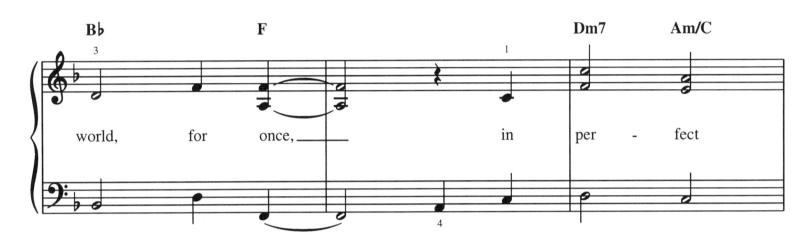

world,   for   once,_____   in   per - fect

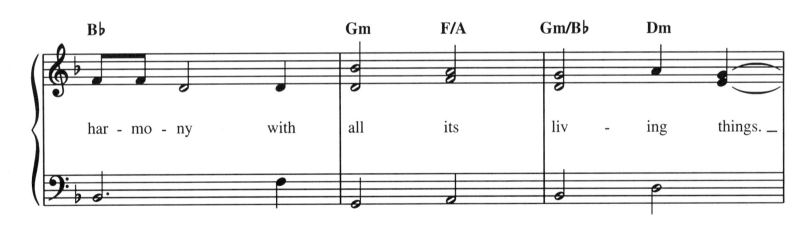

har - mo - ny   with   all   its   liv - ing   things. _

_____
dim.

Simba: So   man - y   things   to
mp

63

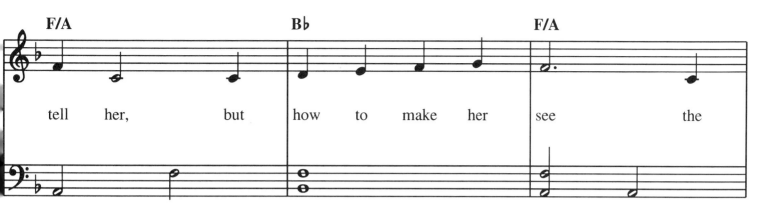

tell her, but how to make her see the

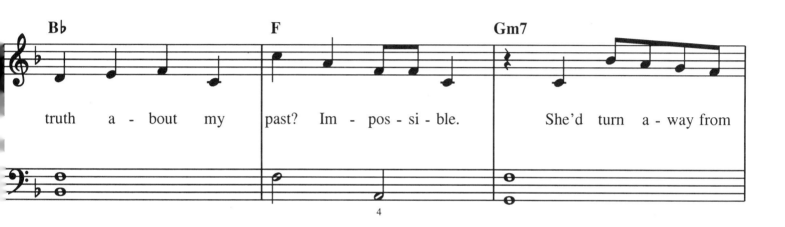

truth a - bout my past? Im - pos - si - ble. She'd turn a - way from

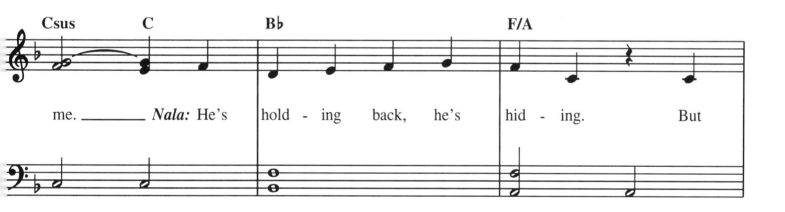

me. _____ *Nala:* He's hold - ing back, he's hid - ing. But

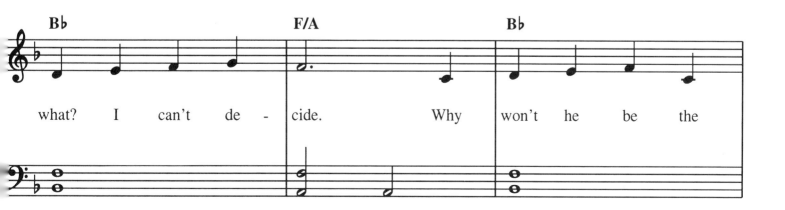

what? I can't de - cide. Why won't he be the

64

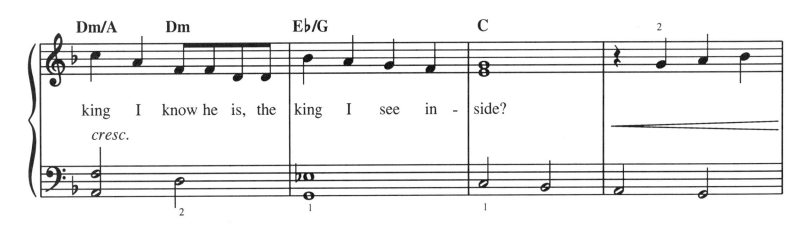

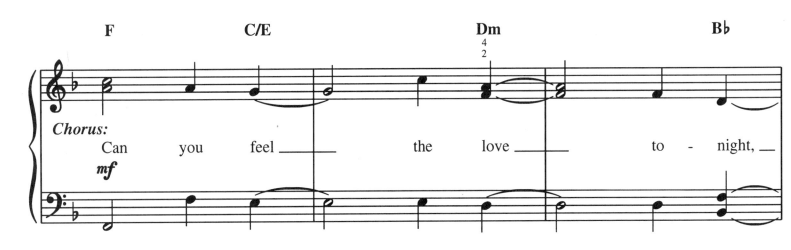

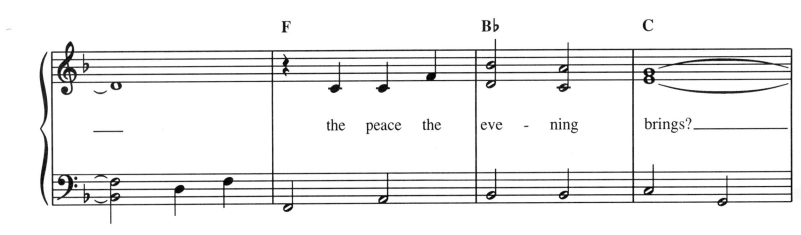

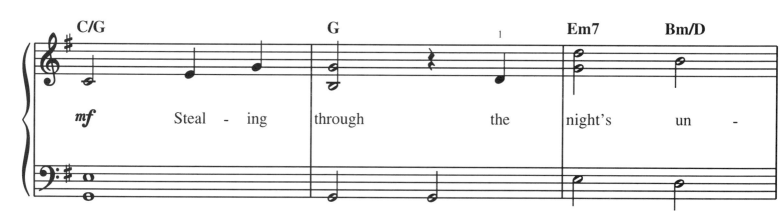

Steal - ing through the night's un -

cer - tain ties, love is where they are. ___

___ *Timon:* And if he

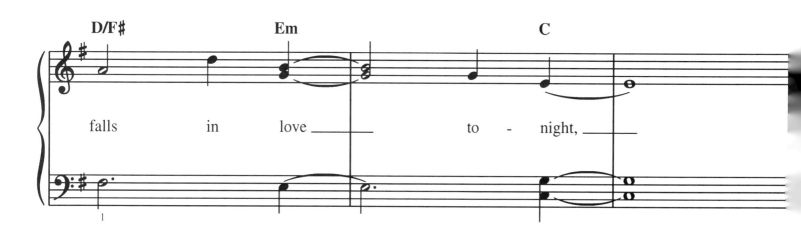

falls in love ___ to - night, ___

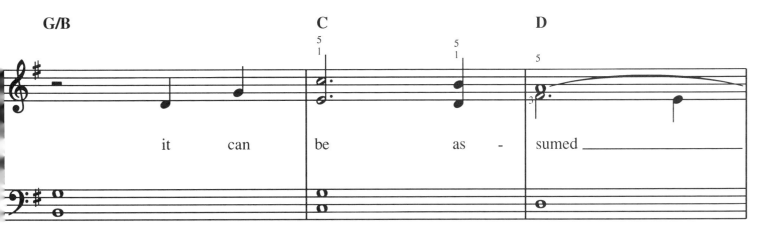

it can be as - sumed _____

___ *Pumbaa:* his care - free days with

us are his - tory, in short, our

Timon And Pumbaa:

rall.

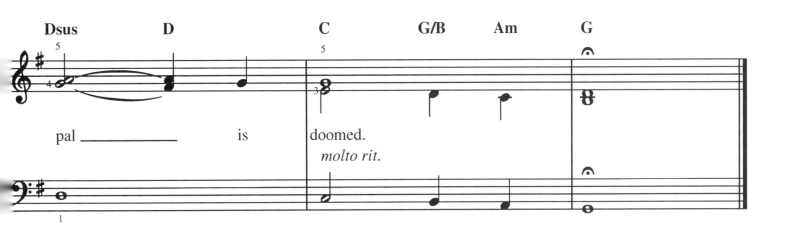

pal _____ is doomed.

molto rit.

DON'T KNOW MUCH

Words and Music by BARRY MANN,
CYNTHIA WEIL and TOM SNOW

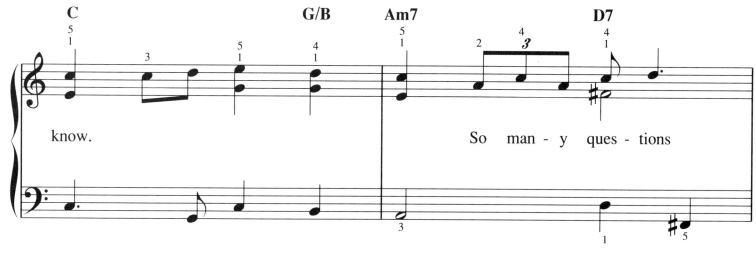

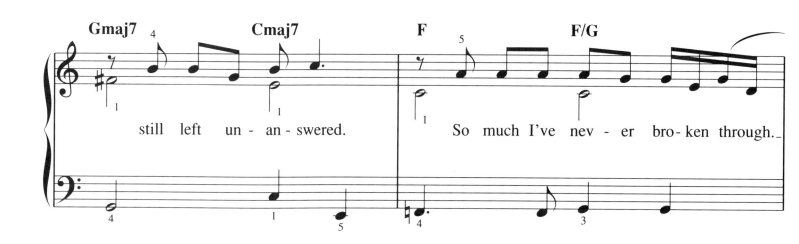

I don't know much, but I know I love you,_____

_____ and that may be_____ all I need to

8a.—

FORREST GUMP - MAIN TITLE
(FEATHER THEME)
from the Paramount Motion Picture FORREST GUMP

Music by ALAN SILVESTRI

Sweetly

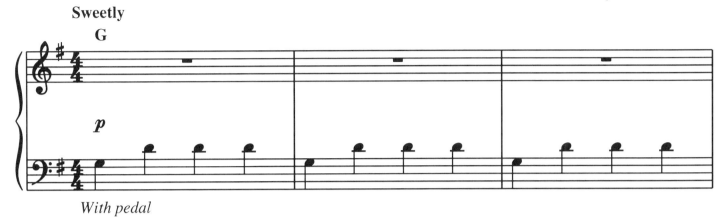

With pedal

sempre legato

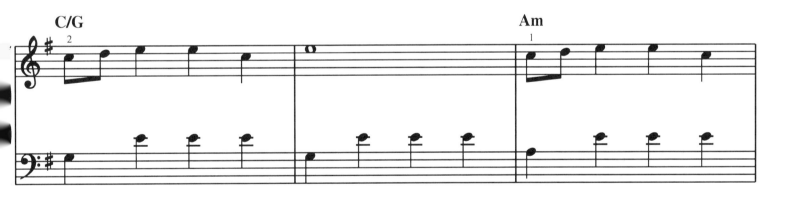

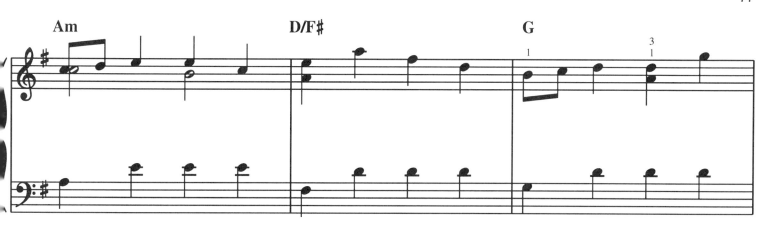

END OF THE ROAD

Words and Music by BABYFACE,
L.A. REID and DARYL SIMMONS

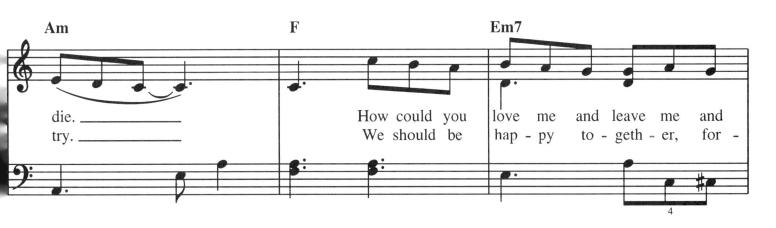

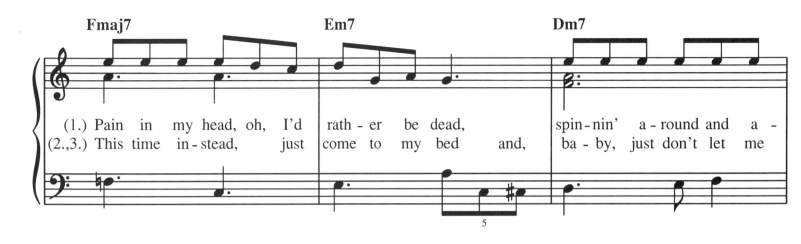

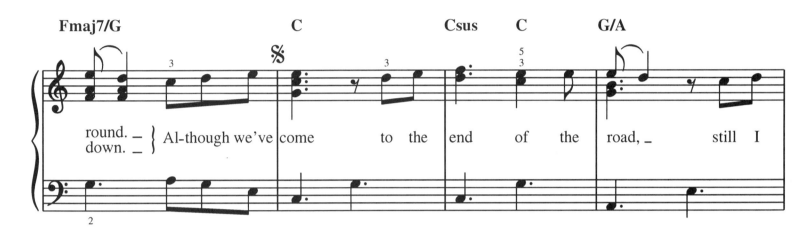

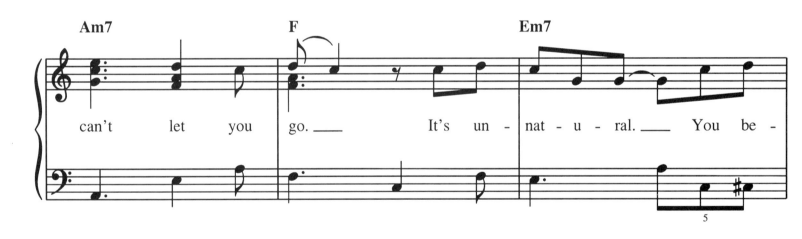

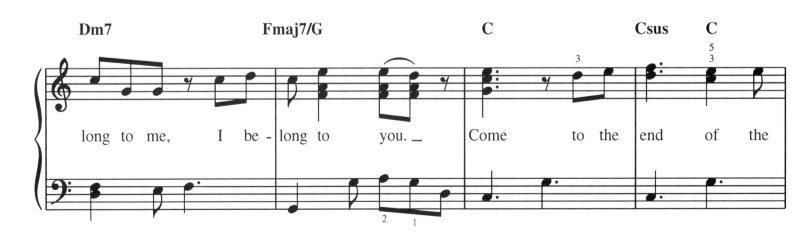

83

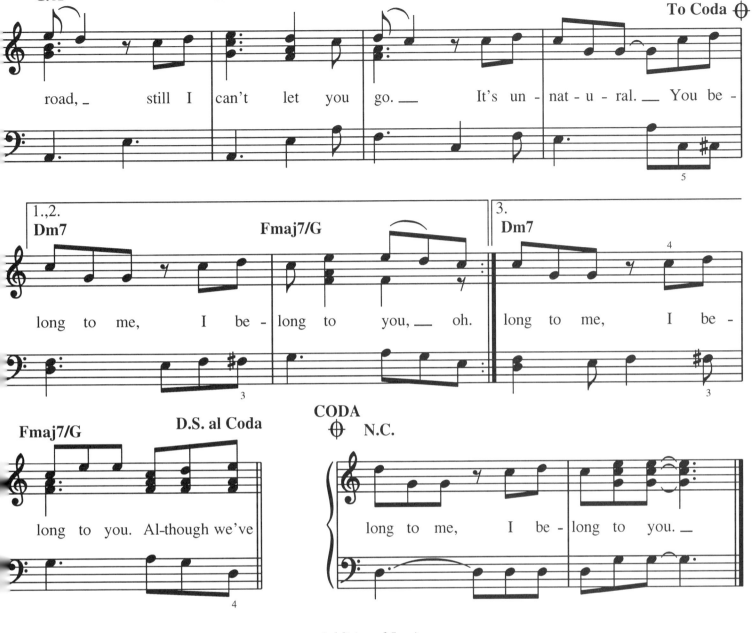

Additional Lyrics

(*Spoken:*) *Girl, I'm here for you.*
All those times at night when you just hurt me,
And just ran out with that other fellow,
Baby, I knew about it.
I just didn't care.
You just don't understand how much I love you, do you?
I'm here for you.
I'm not out to go out there and cheat all night just like you did, baby.
But that's alright, huh, I love you anyway.
And I'm still gonna be here for you 'til my dyin' day, baby.
Right now, I'm just in so much pain, baby.
'Cause you just won't come back to me, will you?
Just come back to me.

Yes, baby, my heart is lonely.
My heart hurts, baby, yes, I feel pain too.
Baby please...

FOREVER IN LOVE

By KENNY G

Tenderly

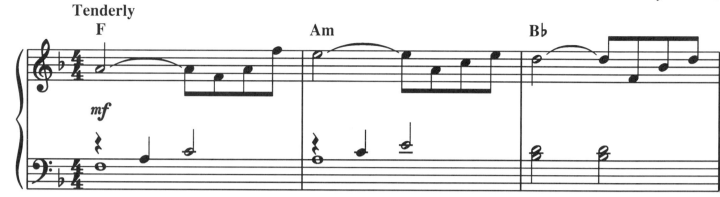

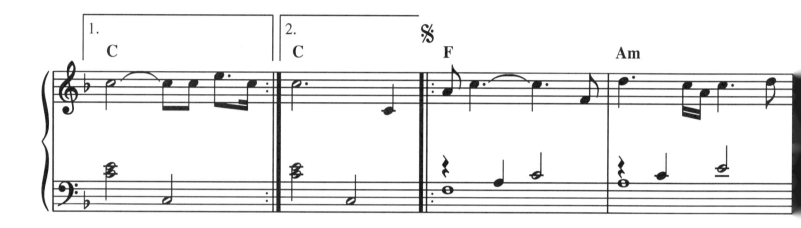

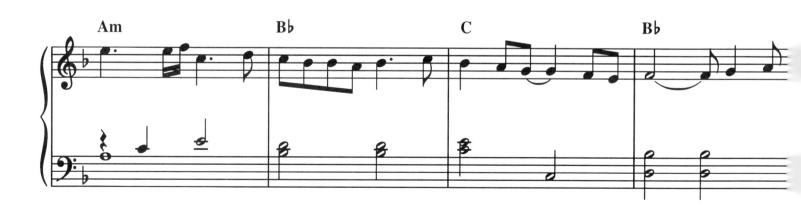

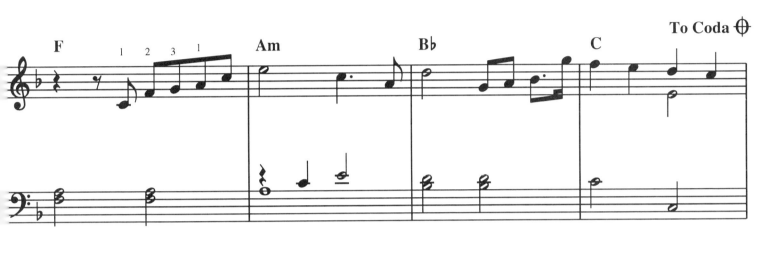

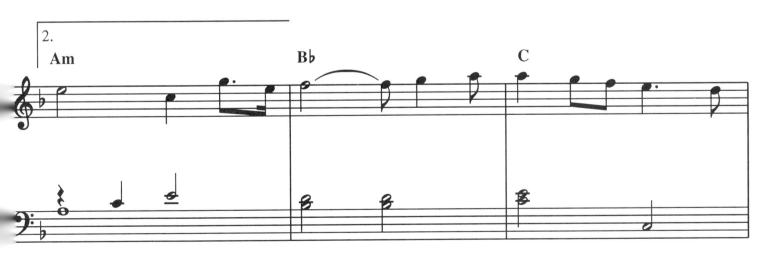

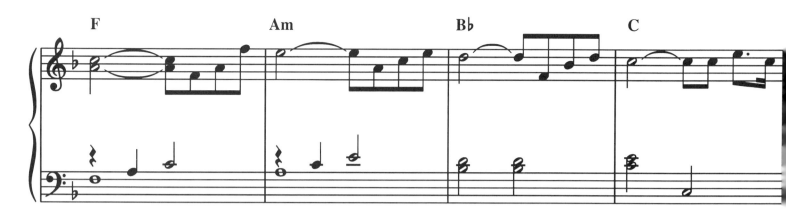

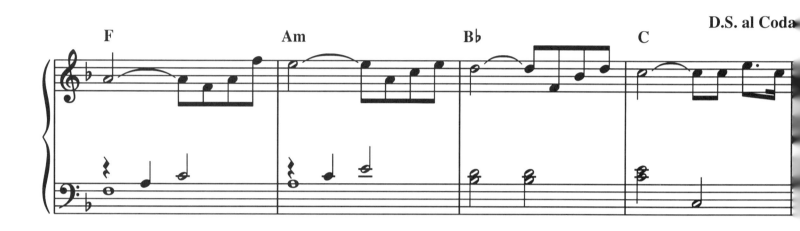

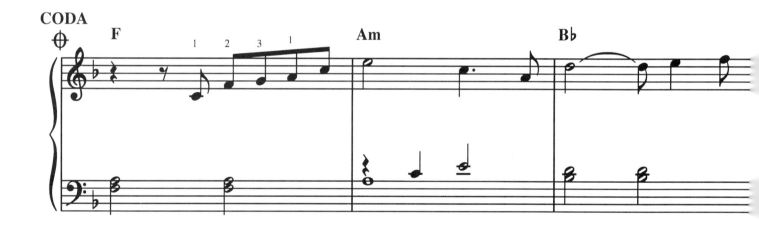

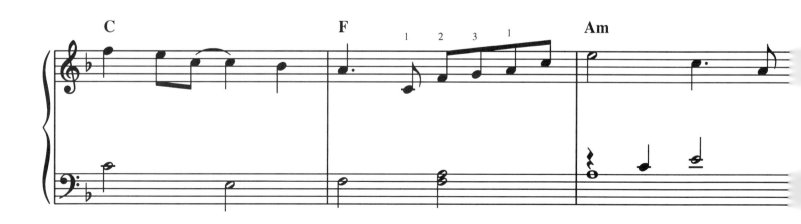

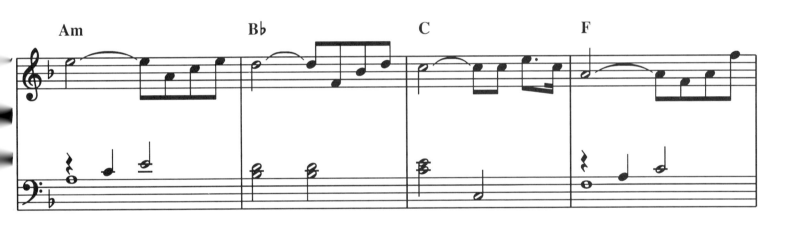

THEME FROM "FRASIER"

from the Paramount Television Series FRASIER

Words by DARRYL PHINNESSEE
Music by BRUCE MILLER

don't know what to do with these tossed sal - ads and scram - bled eggs.

They're call-in' a - gain.

They're call-in' a - gain.

FRIENDS IN LOW PLACES

Words and Music by DEWAYNE BLACKWELL
and EARL BUD LEE

Blame it all on my roots. ___ I
guess I was wrong. ___ I

showed up in boots ___ and ruined your black-tie af-
just don't be-long. ___ But then, I've been there be-

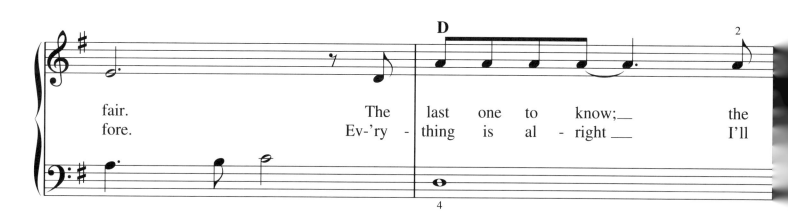

fair. The last one to know; ___ the
fore. Ev'ry-thing is al-right ___ I'll

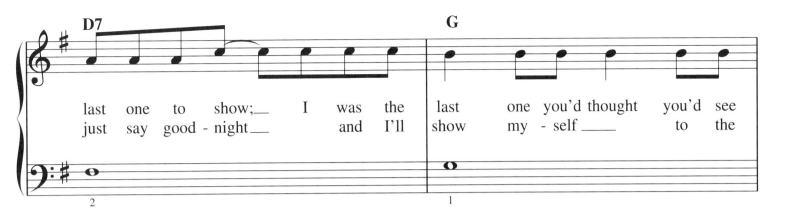

last one to show;___ I was the last one you'd thought you'd see
just say good - night___ and I'll show my - self ____ to the

there. _____ And I saw the sur - prise ___ and the
door. _____ Hey, I did - n't mean ___ to

fear in his eyes___ when I took his glass of cham -
cause a big scene.___ Just give me an ho - ur and

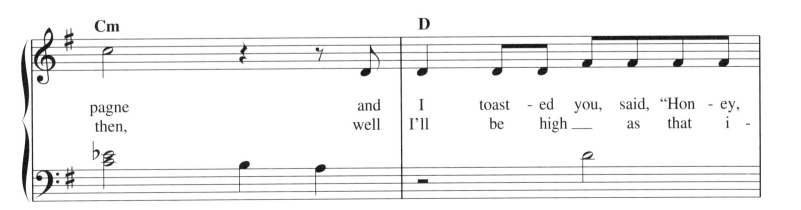

pagne and I toast - ed you, said, "Hon - ey,
then, well I'll be high ___ as that i -

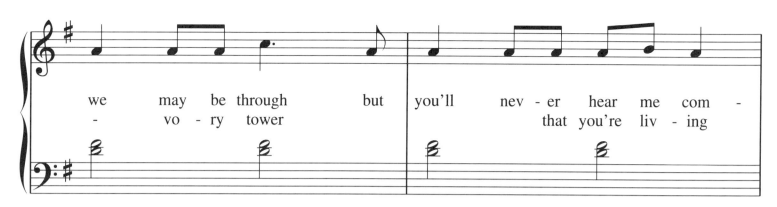

we   may   be through   but   you'll   nev - er   hear   me   com -
- vo - ry tower   that you're   liv - ing

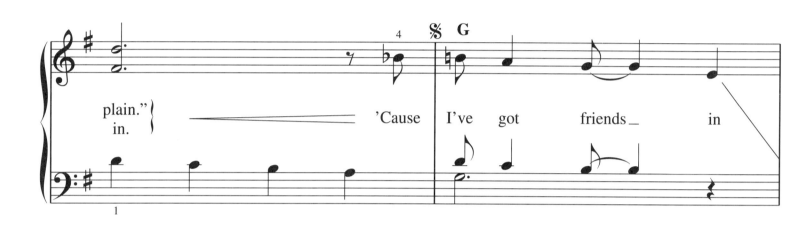

plain."
in.
'Cause   I've   got   friends__   in

low   plac - es, where   the   whis - key   drowns__   and   the

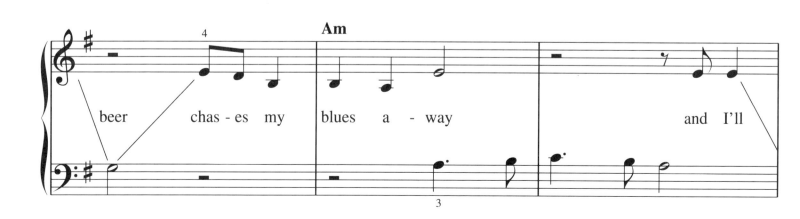

beer   chas - es   my   blues   a - way   and   I'll

be o - kay. Yeah, I'm not big___ on

so - cial grac - es. Think I'll slip on ___ down to the

O - a - sis. Oh, ___ I've got friends in low___

plac - es. ___ Well, I Yeah,

HAVE I TOLD YOU LATELY

Words and Music by
VAN MORRISON

95

like the sun. And at the end of the day

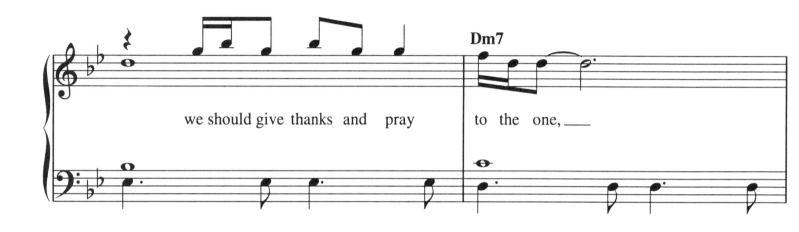

we should give thanks and pray to the one, ___

1. to the one.___ Have I 2. to the one.___ And have I told you late-ly that I

love you? Have I told you there's no one else a - bove you?_____

HERE AND NOW

Words and Music by TERRY STEELE
and DAVID ELLIOT

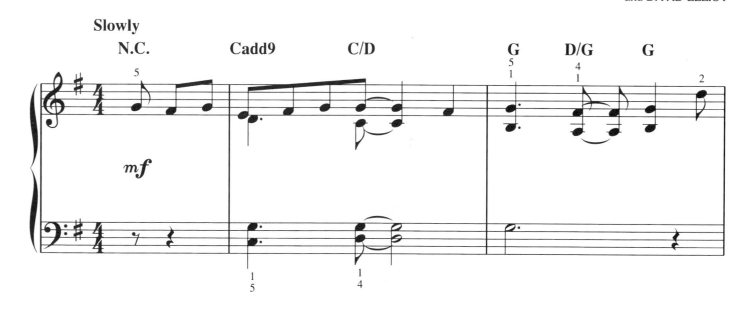

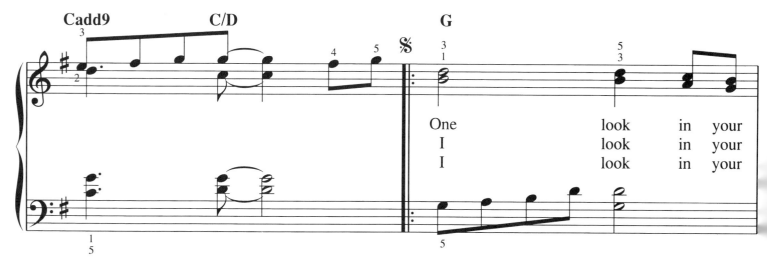

One
I
I

look in your
look in your
look in your

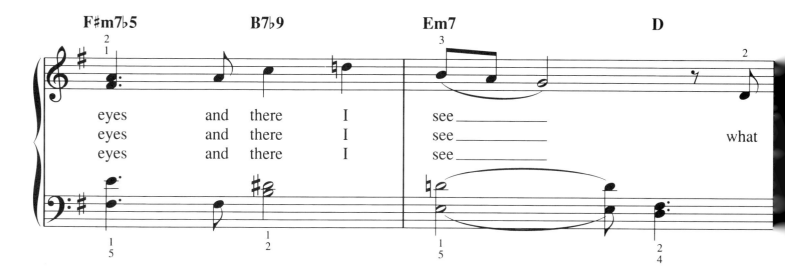

eyes
eyes
eyes

and there
and there
and there

I
I
I

see
see
see

what

100

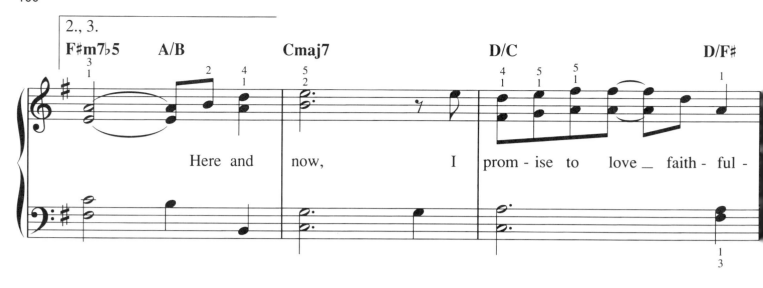

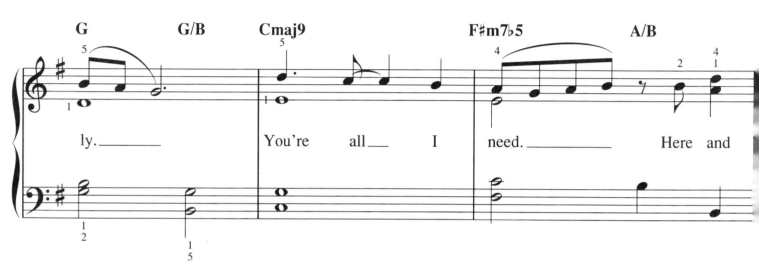

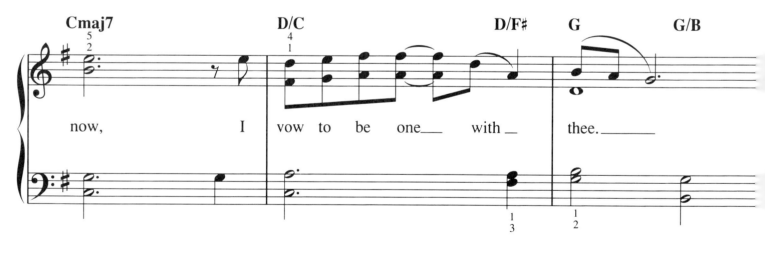

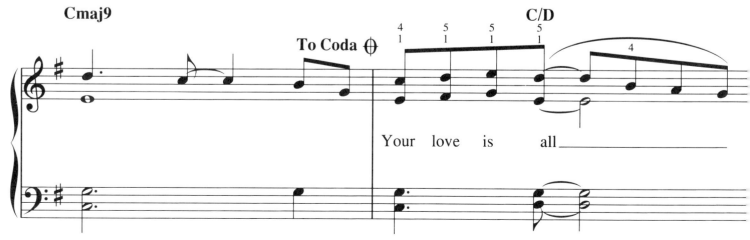

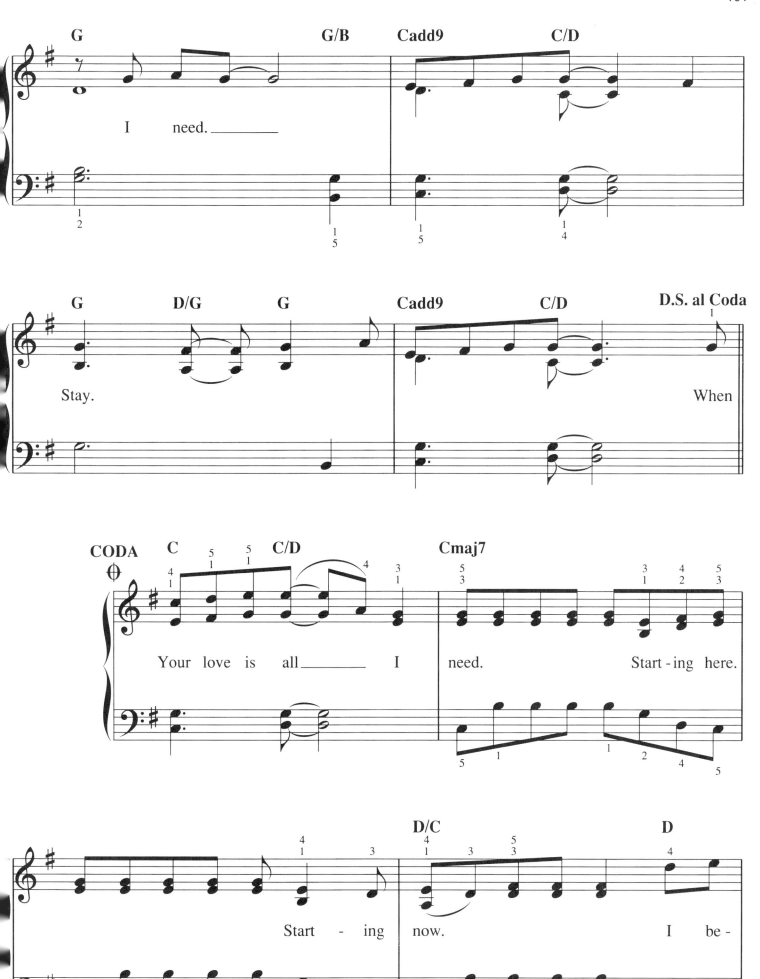

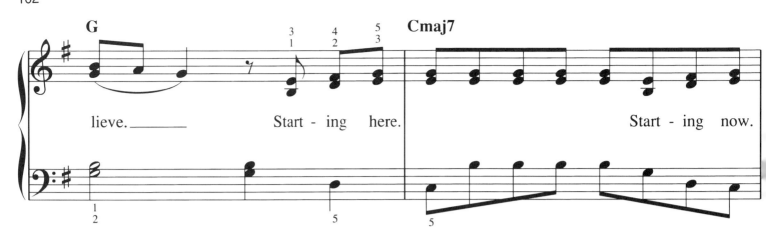

HERO

Words and Music by MARIAH CAREY
and WALTER AFANASIEFF

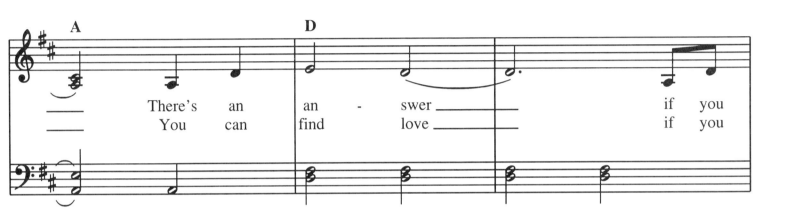

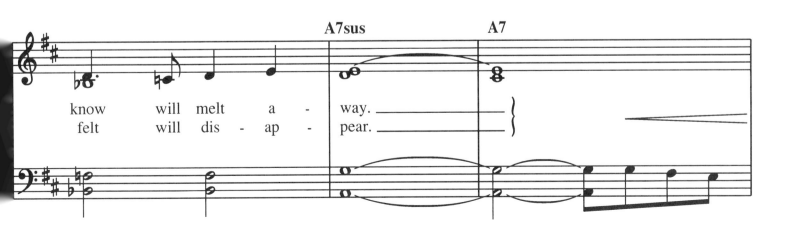

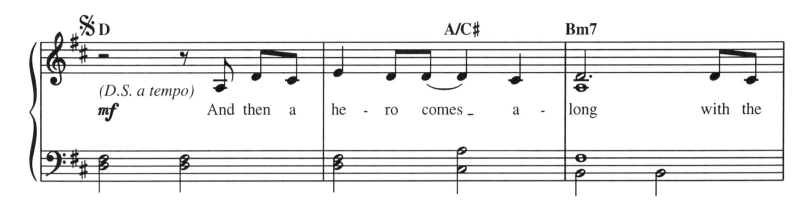

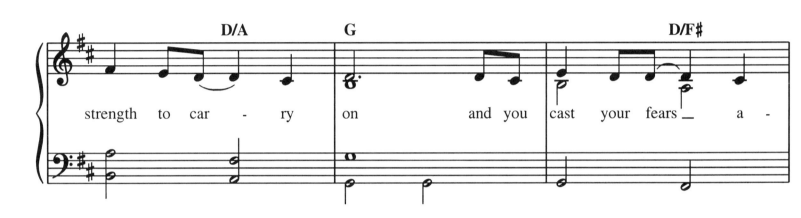

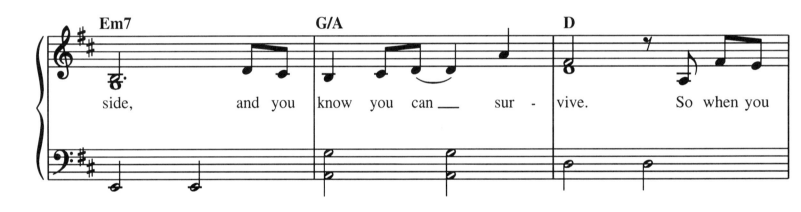

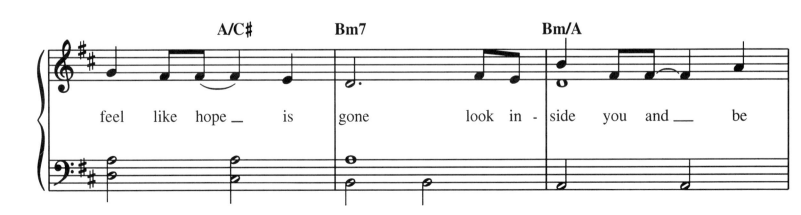

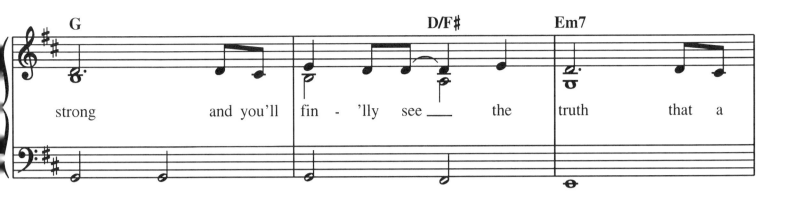

strong   and you'll   fin - 'lly see ___ the   truth   that a

he - ro lies ___ in you.

It's a   you.

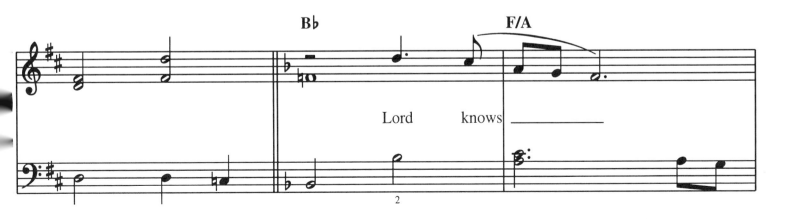

Lord   knows _____

2

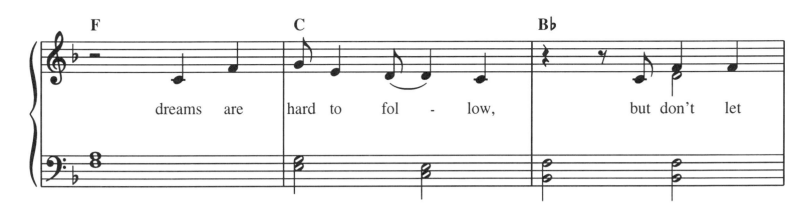

dreams are hard to fol - low, but don't let

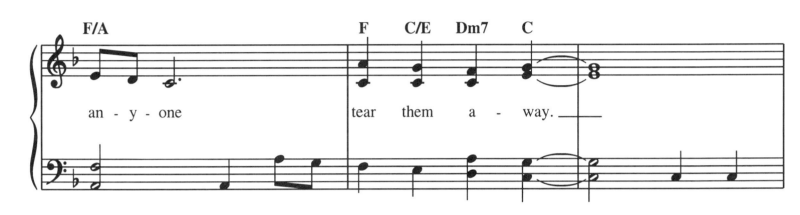

an - y - one tear them a - way.

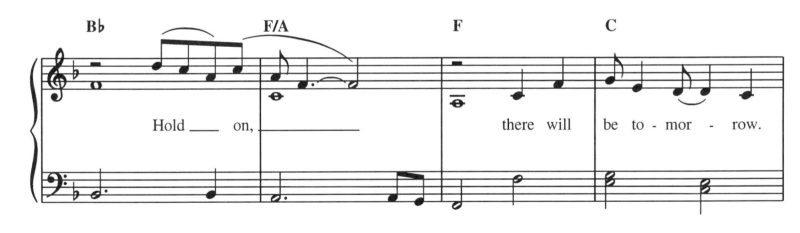

Hold on, there will be to - mor - row.

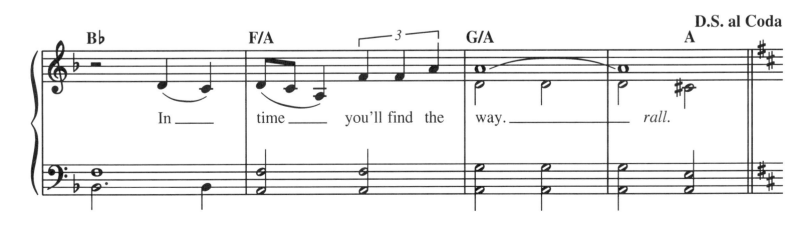

D.S. al Coda

In time you'll find the way. *rall.*

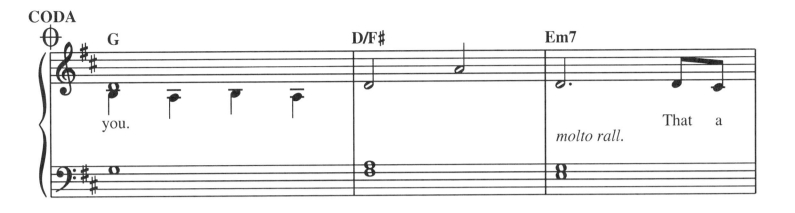

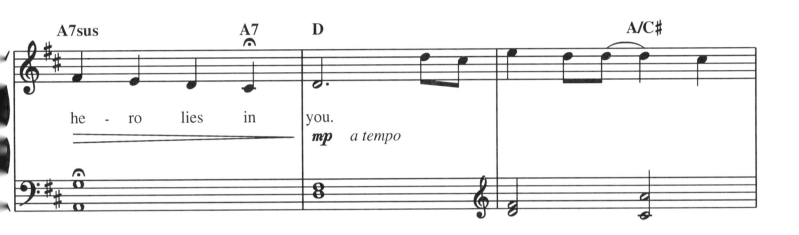

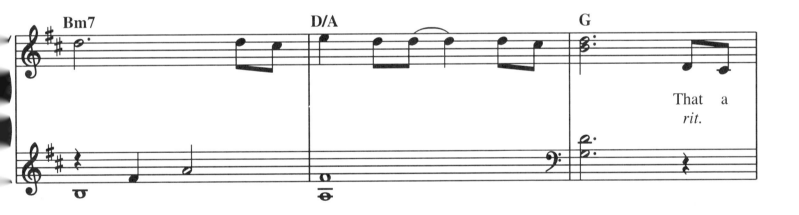

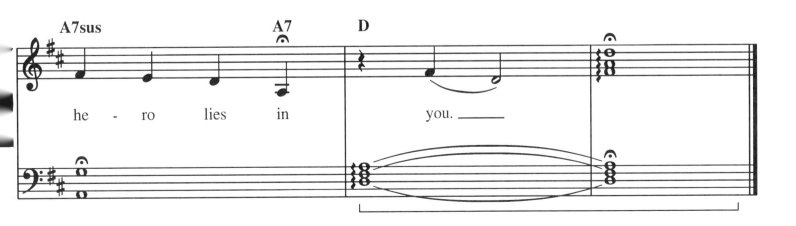

HOLD MY HAND

Words and Music by DARIUS CARLOS RUCKER, EVERETT DEAN FELBER,
MARK WILLIAM BRYAN and JAMES GEORGE SONEFELD

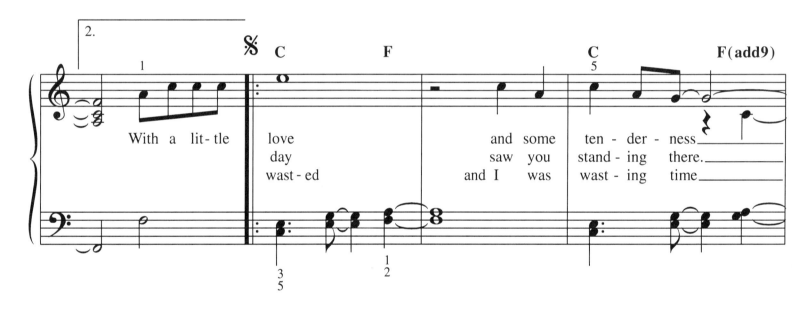

With a lit-tle love
day
wast-ed

and some
saw you
and I was

ten-der-ness
stand-ing there.
wast-ing time

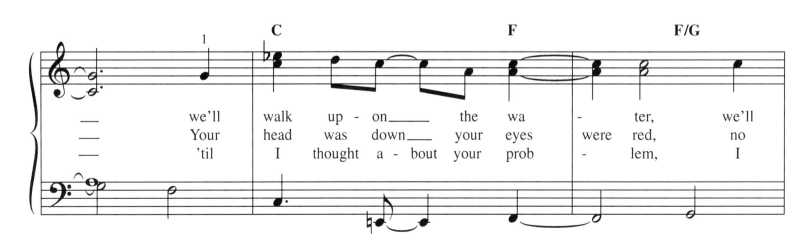

we'll
Your
'til

walk
head
I

up - on
was down
thought a - bout

the wa
your eyes
your prob

-
ter,
were red,
lem,

we'll
no
I

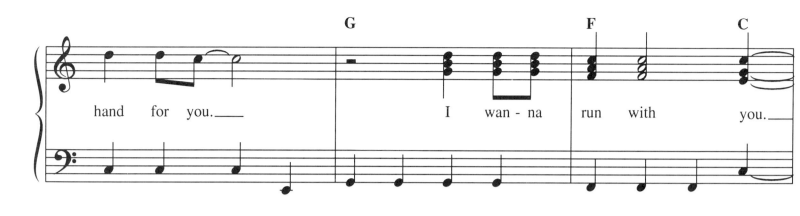

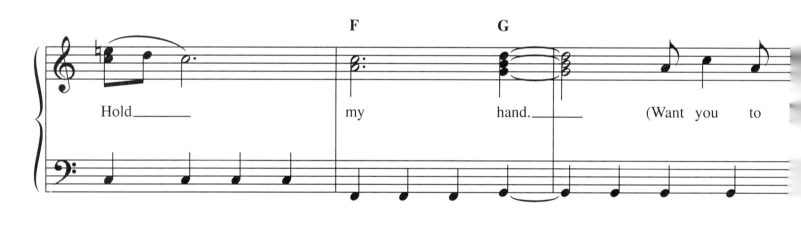

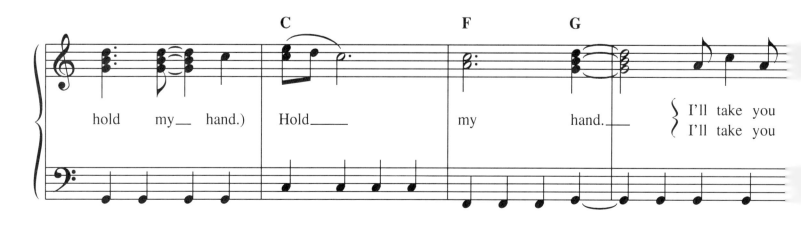

113

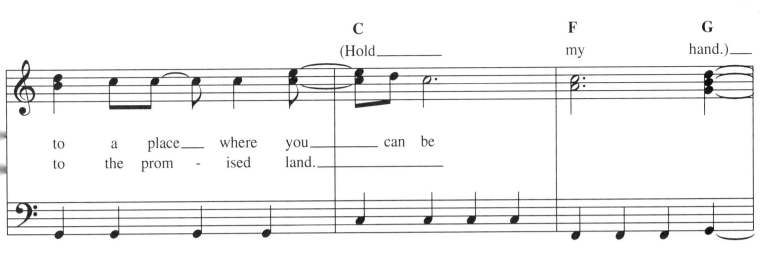

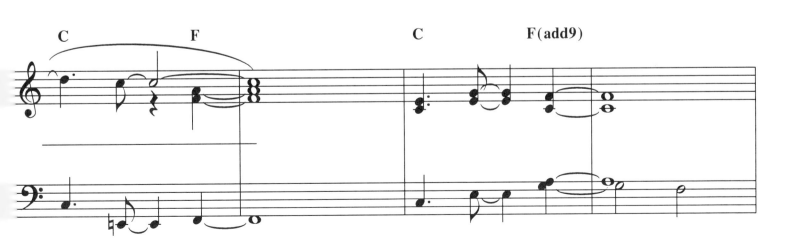

114

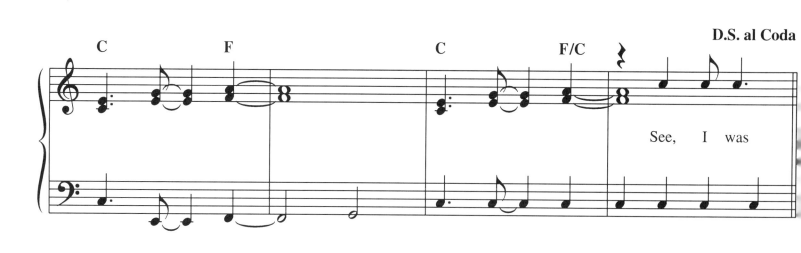

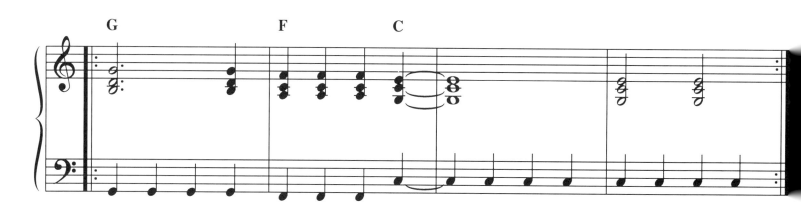

116

oh,_____ no, no, no. I wan-na love you____ the

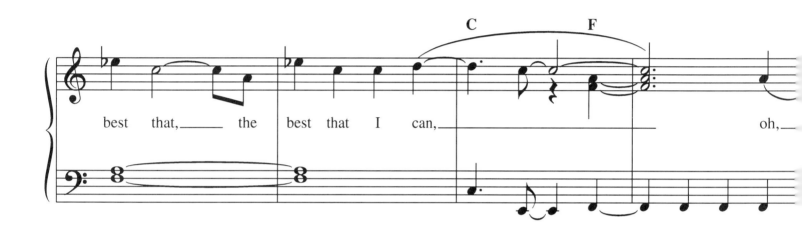

best that,____ the best that I can,____ oh,__

_ the__ best__ I can,____

_ oh,__ the__ best__ I can.

I'D DO ANYTHING FOR LOVE
(BUT I WON'T DO THAT)

Words and Music by
JIM STEINMAN

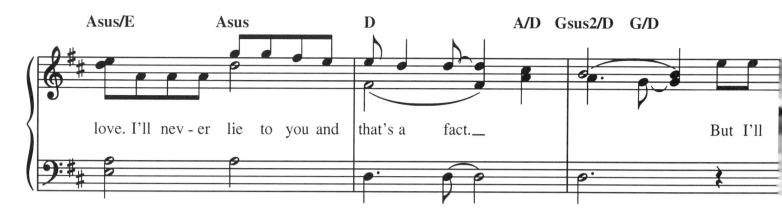

love. I'll nev - er lie to you and that's a fact.___ But I'll

nev - er for - get ___ the way you feel right now,___ oh ___

no, no ___ way. And I would do an - y - thing ___ for

love, but I won't do that. No I won't do

that.

Gmaj7   **A**

Bm   **G**

Some days   it   don't come   eas - y,   some days   it
Some nights you're   breath - ing   fire,_   some nights you're
Some days   I   pray for   si - lence,   some days   I

Em7

don't come   hard._   Some days it don't   come at   all __ and
carved in   ice. __   Some nights are like   noth-ing   I've ev - er
pray for   soul. _   Some days I just   pray to   the God   of

an - y - thing _ for love. Oh, I would do an - y - thing _ for
that's a fact. I would do an - y - thing _ for

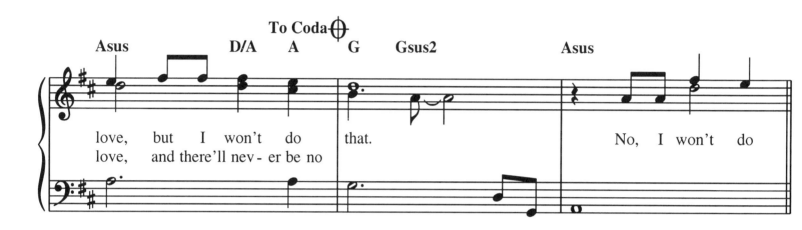

To Coda

love, but I won't do that. No, I won't do
love, and there'll nev - er be no

Tempo I

that. I would _ do an - y - thing _ for love, an - y - thing

you've been dream - ing of, but I ____ just won't ____ do ____

123

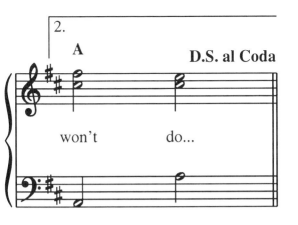

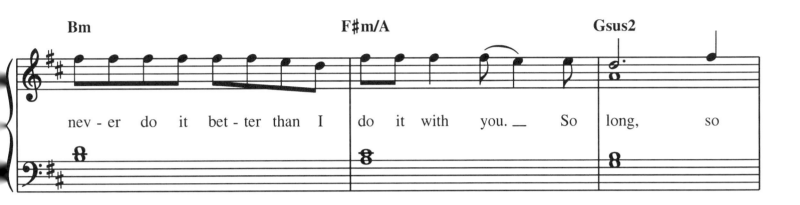

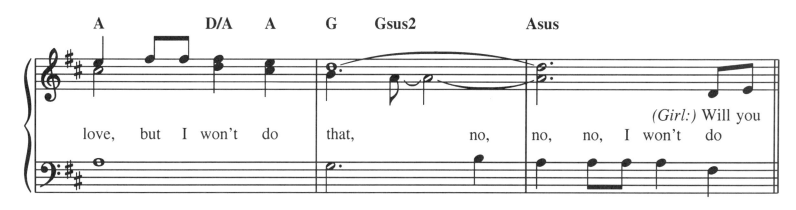

love,   but   I won't do   that,   no,   no,   no, I won't do
                                                                    (Girl:) Will you

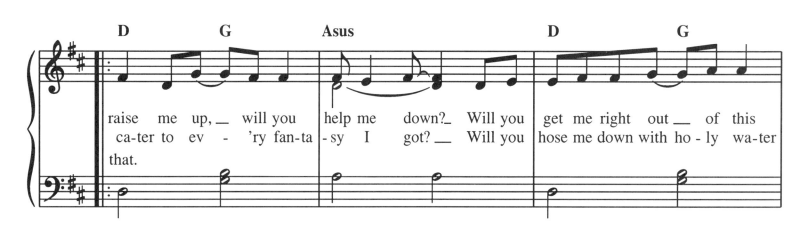

raise   me   up, __ will you   help me   down?__ Will you   get me right out __ of this
ca-ter to ev - 'ry fan-ta -sy I   got? __ Will you   hose me down with ho - ly wa-ter
that.

god - for - sak - en town? Will you   make it   all   a   lit - tle less   cold? *(Boy:)* I   can do
if   I get too hot? Will you   take me plac - es I've nev - er   gone? *(Boy:)* I   can do

1.

2.

that,   oh ___   no ___ I can do
that,   oh ___   no ___ I can do
                              (Girl:) Will you

I know the ter - ri - tor - y, I've been a-round. It - 'll all turn to dust _ and we'll
that.

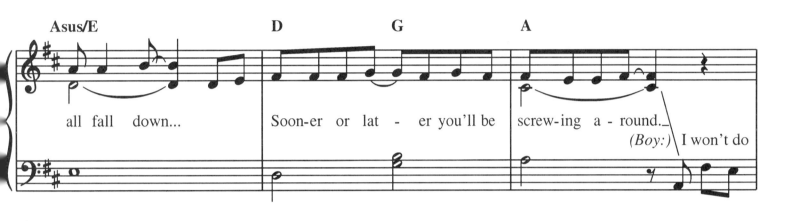

all fall down... Soon-er or lat - er you'll be screw-ing a - round. _
(Boy:) I won't do

that. No, I won't do An - y - thing _ for that.

love, but I won't do that.

HOW AM I SUPPOSED TO LIVE WITHOUT YOU

Words and Music by MICHAEL BOLTON
and DOUG JAMES

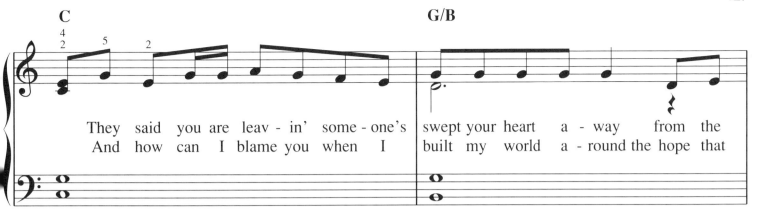

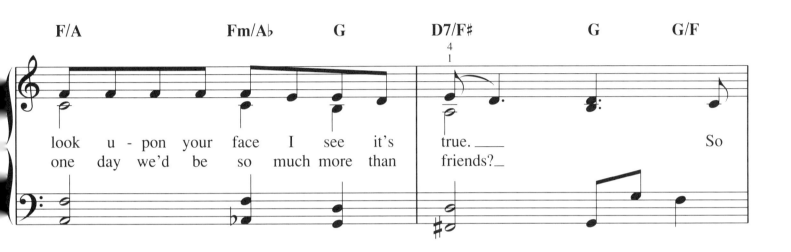

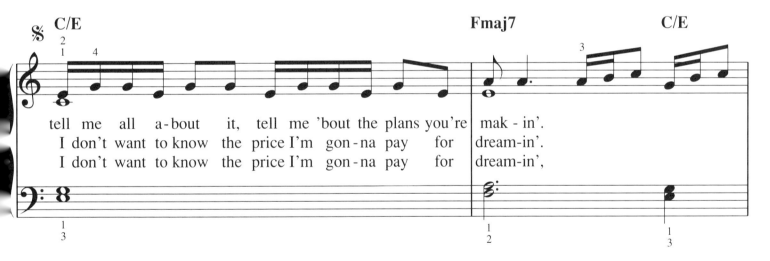

128

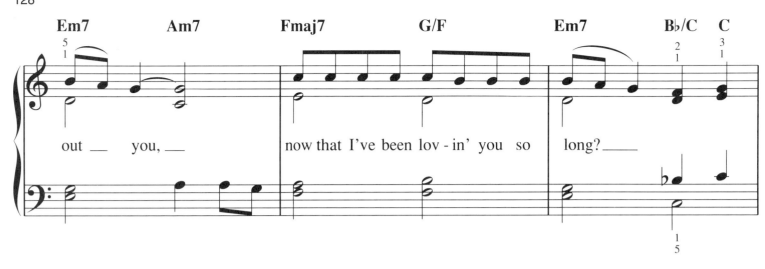

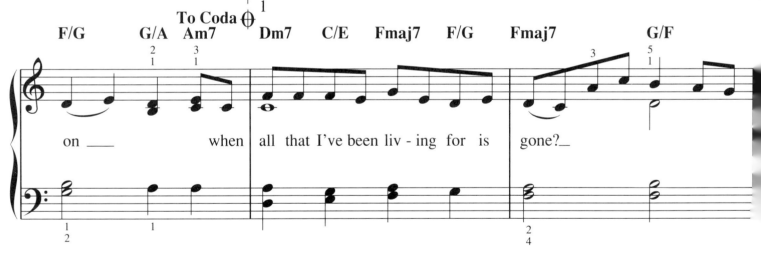

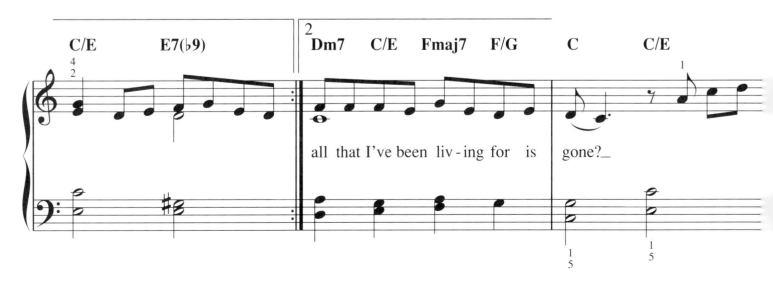

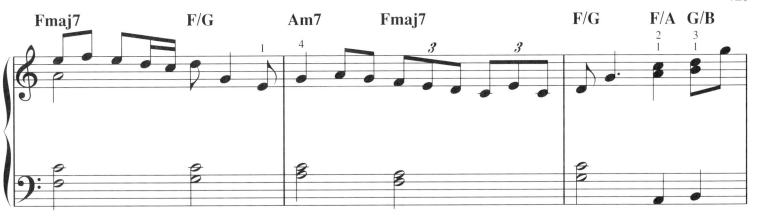

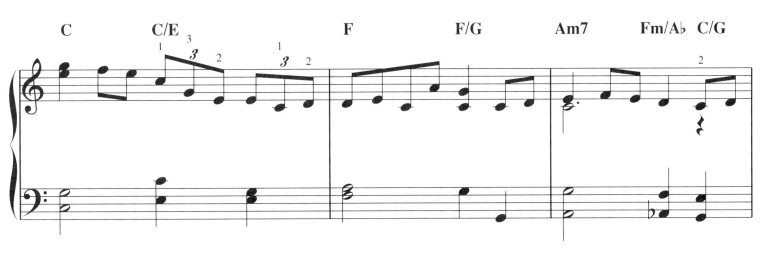

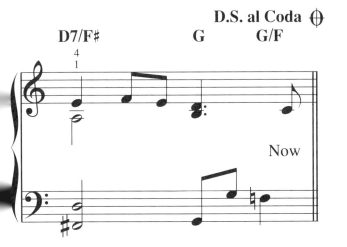

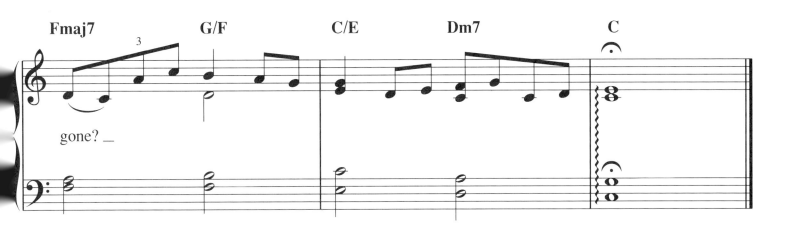

I BELIEVE

Words and Music by JEFFREY PENCE,
ELIOT SLOAN and EMOSIA

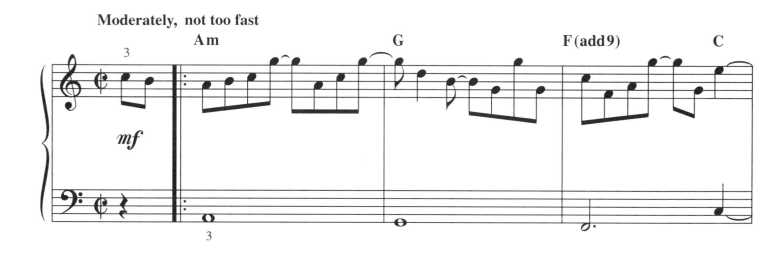

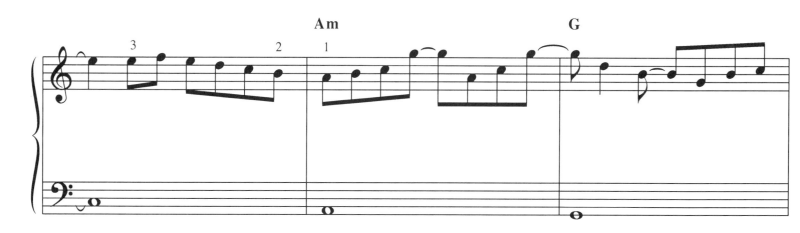

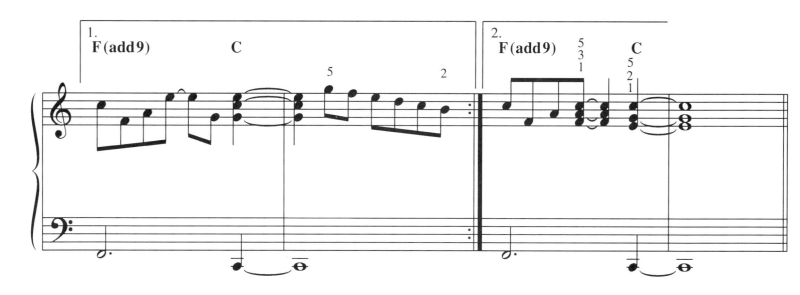

131

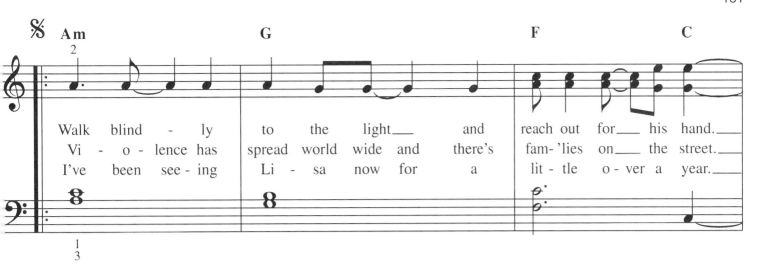

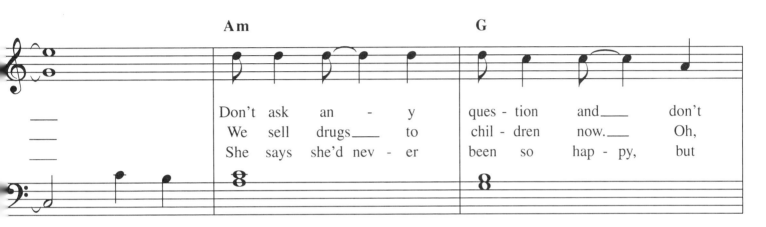

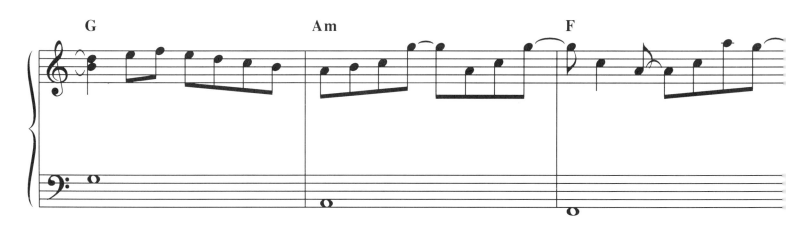

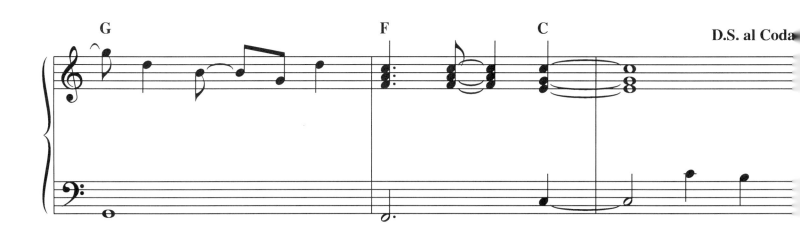

___ 'Cause she be - lieves___ that love___ will see___ it through___ and

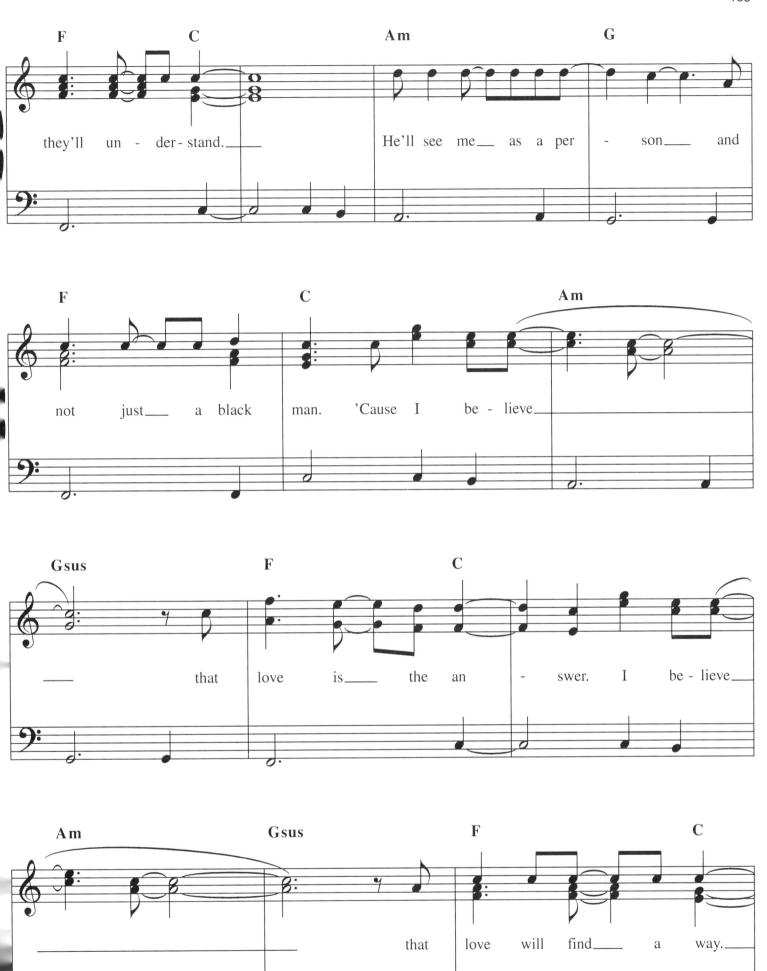

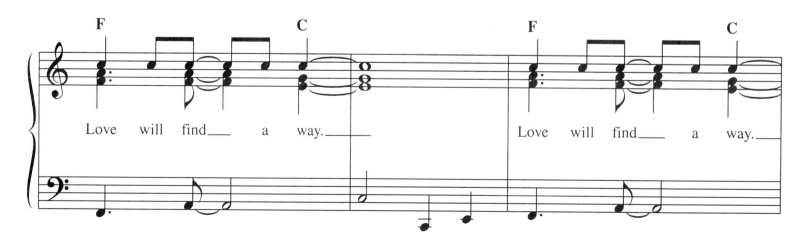

Love will find___ a way.___

I DON'T HAVE THE HEART

Words and Music by ALLAN RICH
and JUD FRIEDMAN

MCA music publishing

139

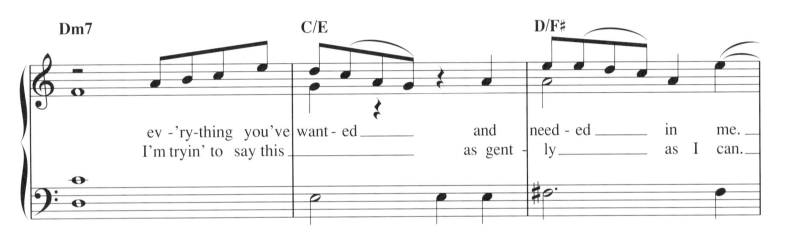

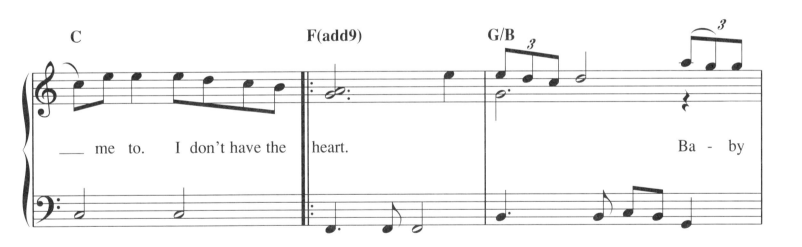

I'LL MAKE LOVE TO YOU

Words and Music by
BABYFACE

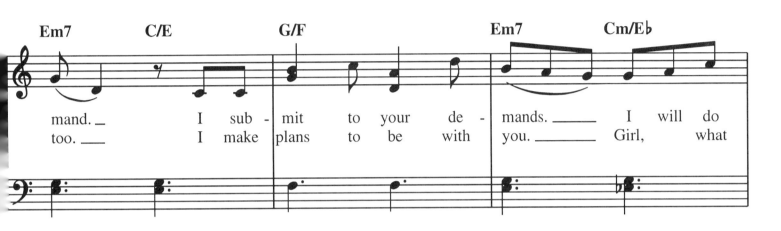

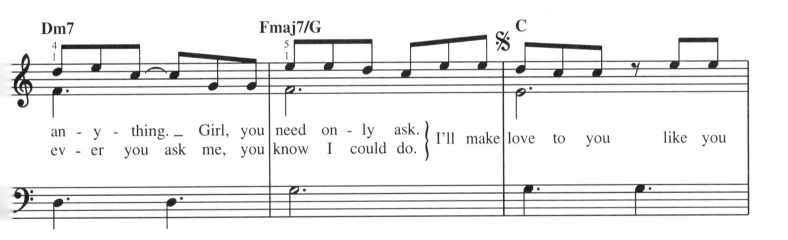

144

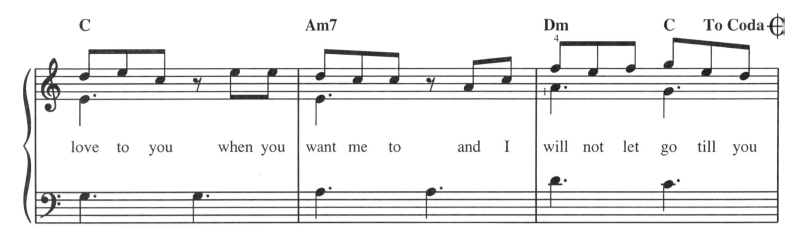

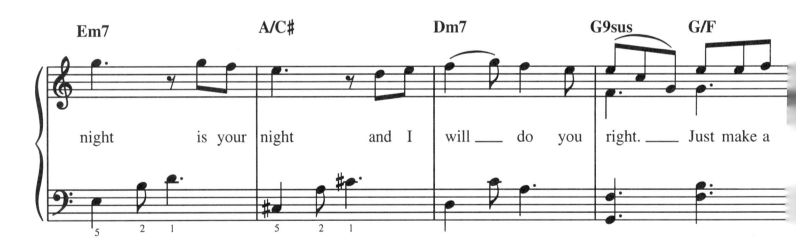

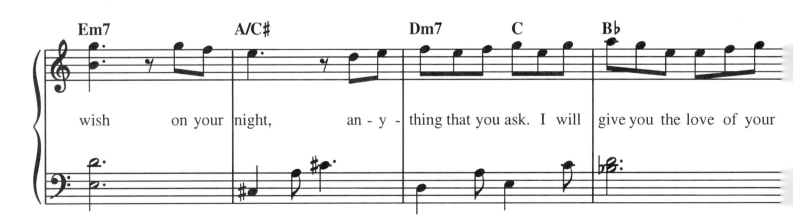

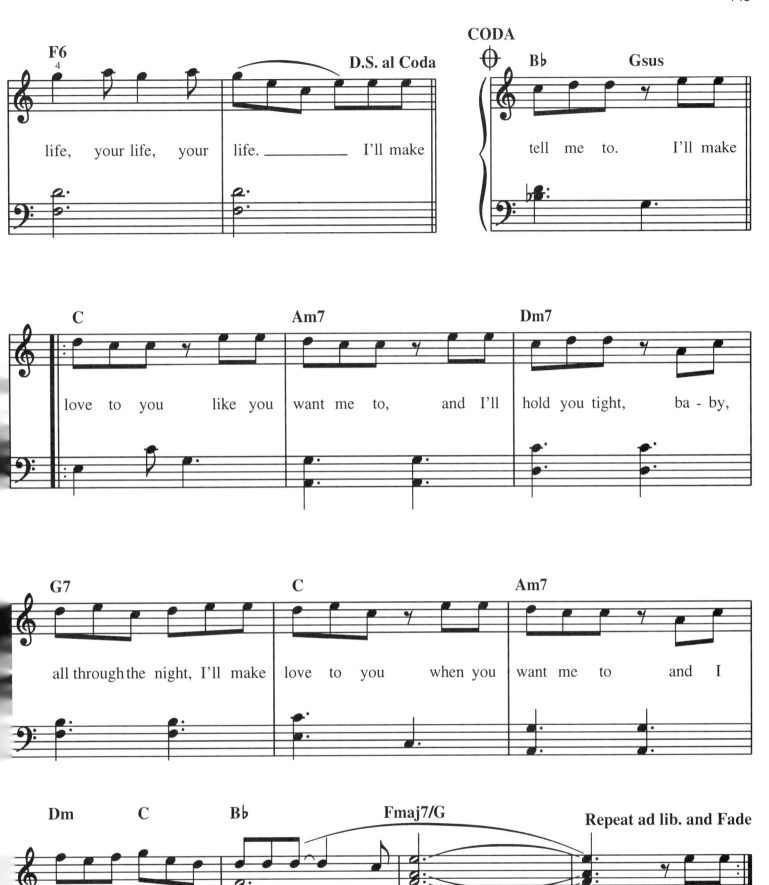

IN THE STILL OF THE NITE
(I'll Remember)

Words and Music by
FRED PARRIS

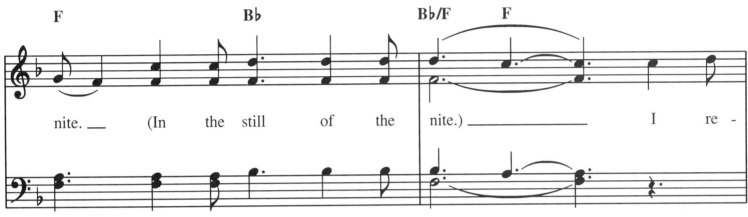

keep your pre - cious love. _____ So, _ be- fore _____ the ___

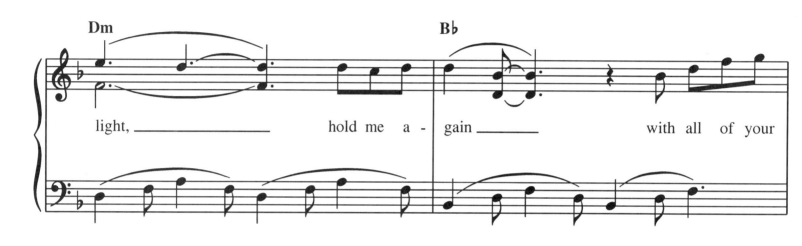

light, _____ hold me a - gain _____ with all of your

might _____ in the still _____ of ___ the nite. (In the still of the

nite.) _____ (Shoo wop shoo wah, shoo wop shoo wah,

150

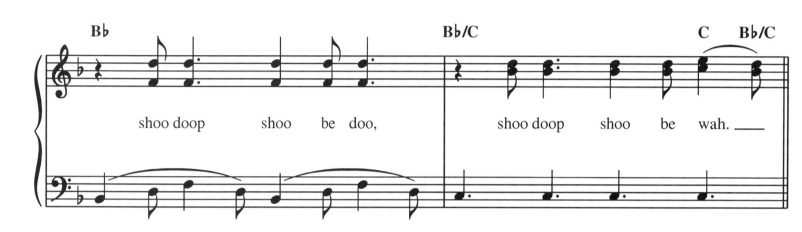

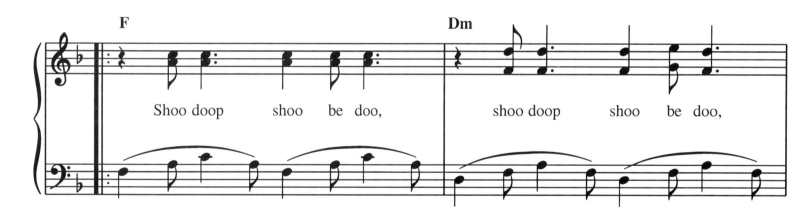

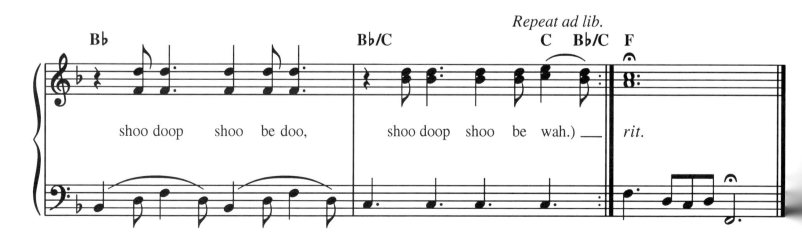

OPPOSITES ATTRACT

Words and Music by
OLIVER LEIBER

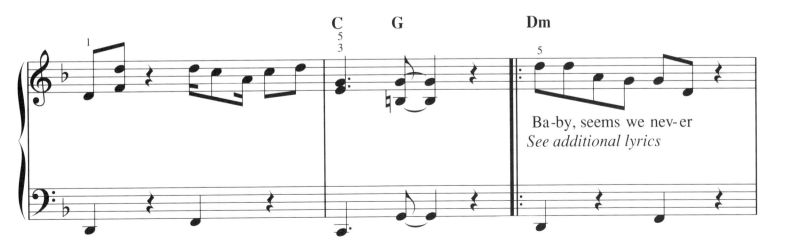

Ba-by, seems we nev-er
See additional lyrics

ev - er a - gree.____ you like the mo - vies and I like T. __ V.

I take things ser - i - ous and you take them light. I go to bed ear - ly, and I

par - ty all night. __ our friends are say - in' we ain't gon-na last. ____

'Cause I move slow-ly, and ba - by I'm__ fast. I like it qui - et and

153

I like to shout. But when we get to - geth-er it just all works out. _ I take

two steps for-ward, I take two steps back. _ we come to - geth-er 'cause

op - po- sites at-tract and you know it ain't fic-tion, just a nat-u - ral fact. _____

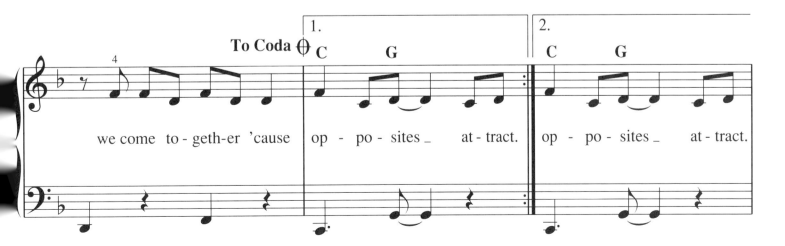

we come to - geth-er 'cause op - po - sites _ at - tract. op - po - sites _ at - tract.

Two steps for-ward, I take two steps back. _ We come to - geth-er 'cause

op - po-sites at-tract and you know it ain't fic-tion, just a nat - u - ral fact. _____

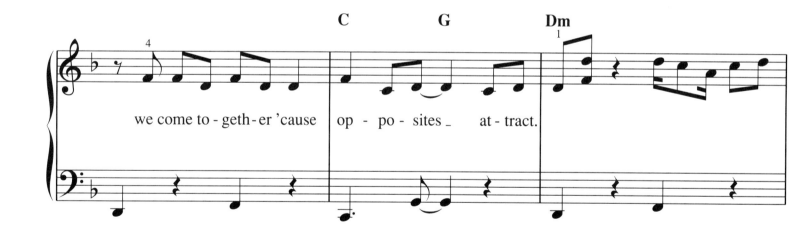

we come to - geth-er 'cause op - po - sites _ at - tract.

D.S. al Coda

155

CODA

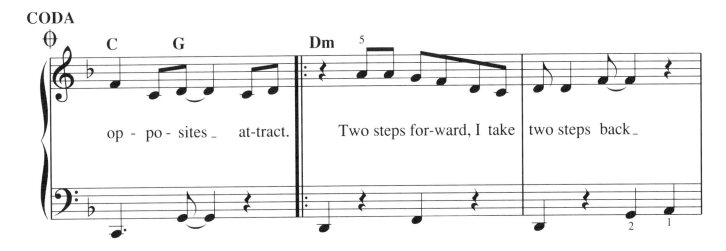

op - po - sites _ at-tract. | Two steps for-ward, I take | two steps back _

we come to-geth-er 'cause | op- po-sites at-tract. And you know | it ain't fic-tion, just a

nat - u - ral fact. _____ | We come to-geth-er 'cause | op - po - sites _ at - tract.

Additional Lyrics

3. Who'd a thought we could be lovers.
She makes the bed and he steals the covers.
She likes it neat and he makes a mess.
I take it easy; baby, I get obsessed.

4. She's got the money, and he's always broke.
I don't like cigarettes, and I like to smoke.
Things in common, just ain't a one.
But when we get together we have nothin' but fun.
(To Chorus:)

5. Baby, ain't it somethin' how we lasted this long.
You and me provin' everyone wrong.
Don't think we'll ever get our differences patched.
Don't really matter 'cause we're perfectly matched.
(To Chorus:)

LOSING MY RELIGION

Words and Music by BILL BERRY, PETER BUCK,
MIKE MILLS, MICHAEL STIPE

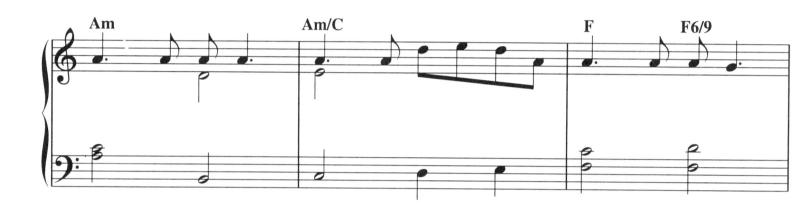

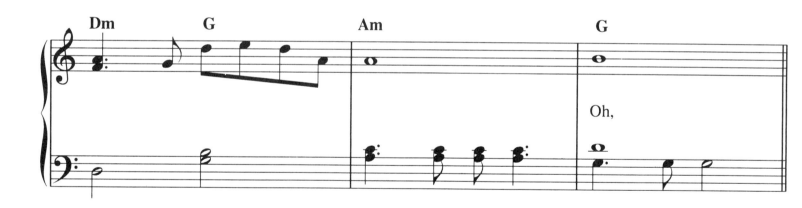

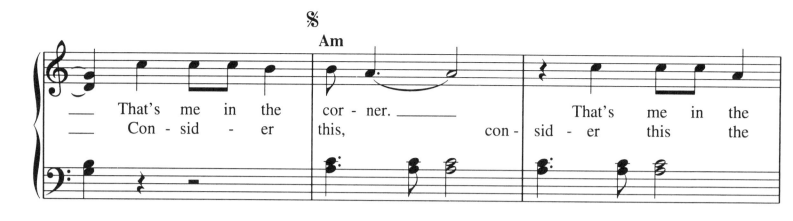

%
Am

That's me in the cor - ner. _____ That's me in the
Con - sid - er this, con - sid - er this the

Em   Am

spot - light los - ing my re - li - gion _____
hint of the cen-tu-ry. Con - sid - er this the slip

Em

try - ing to keep up _____ with you and I
that brought me to my knees failed.

Am   Em

don't know if I can do it. _____ Oh no I've
What if all these fan - ta - sies come flail - ing a -

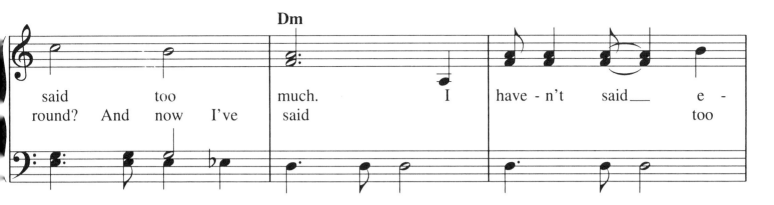

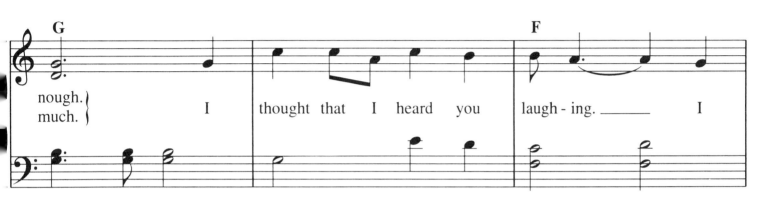

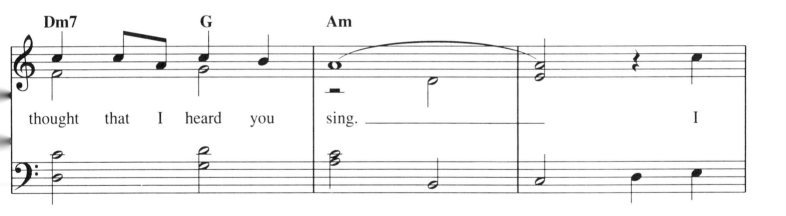

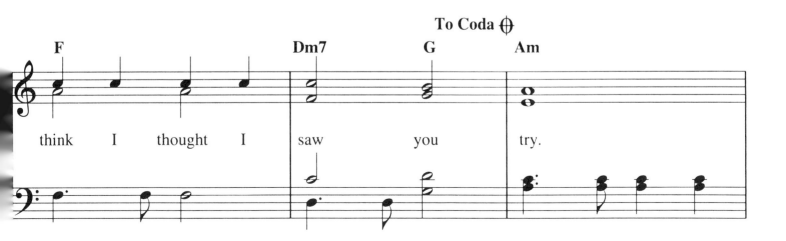

160

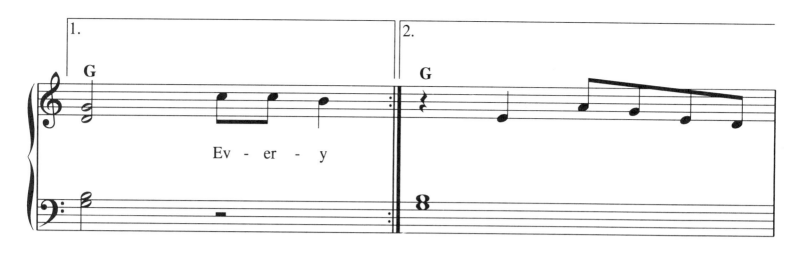

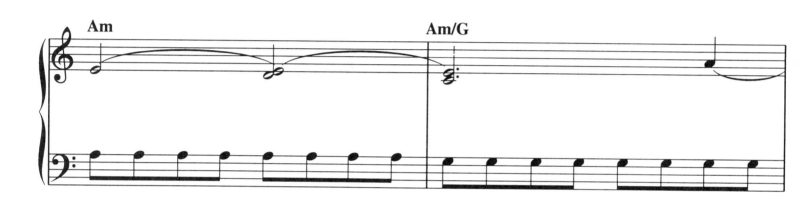

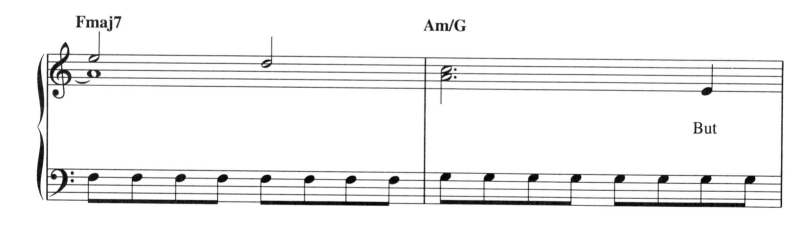

But

that was just a dream. That was just a

161

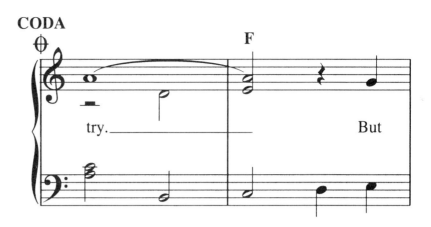

ONE SWEET DAY

Words and Music by MARIAH CAREY, WALTER AFANASIEFF, SHAWN STOCKMAN,
MICHAEL McCARY, NATHAN MORRIS and WANYA MORRIS

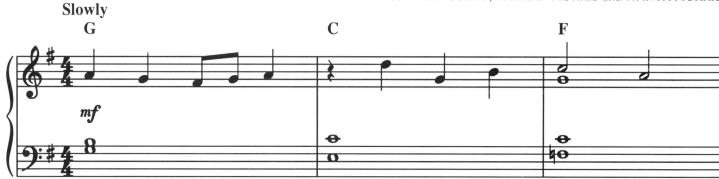

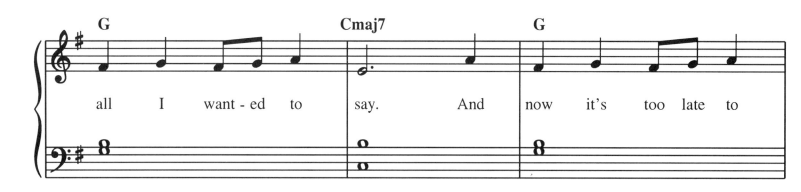

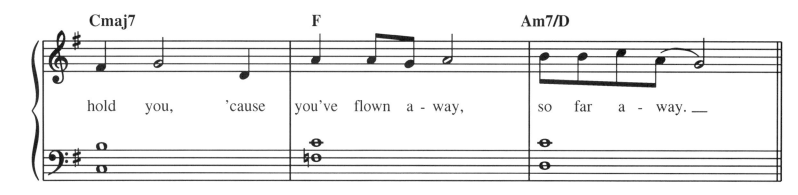

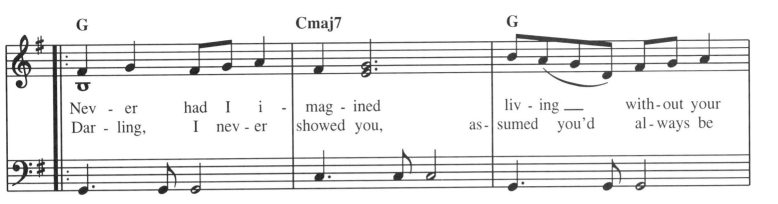

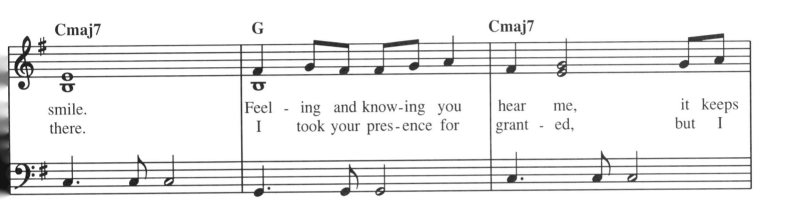

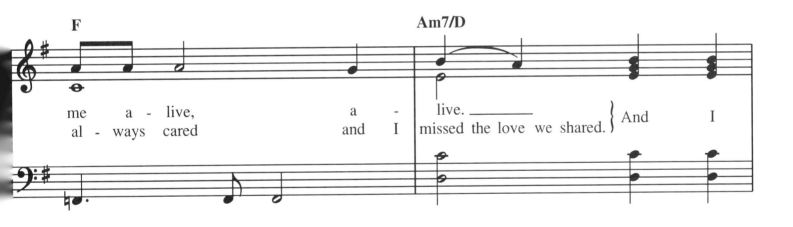

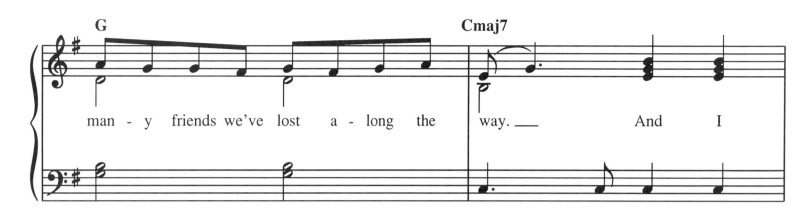

man - y friends we've lost a - long the way. ___ And I

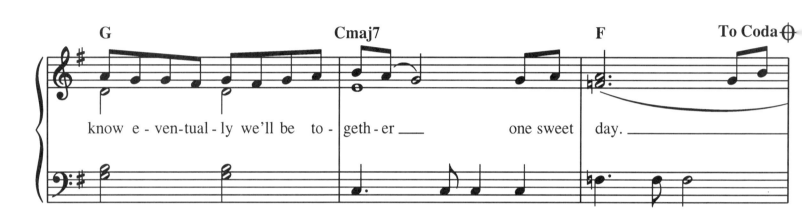

know e - ven-tual - ly we'll be to - geth - er ___ one sweet day. _____

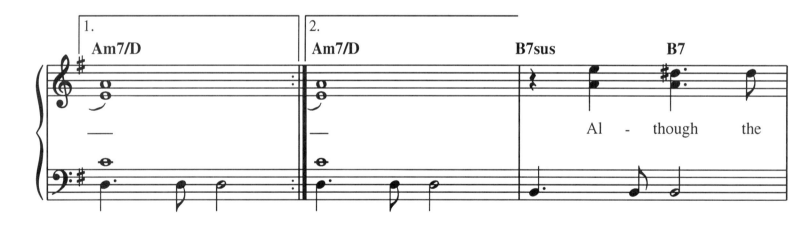

1.
Am7/D   2. Am7/D   B7sus   B7

___   ___   Al - though the

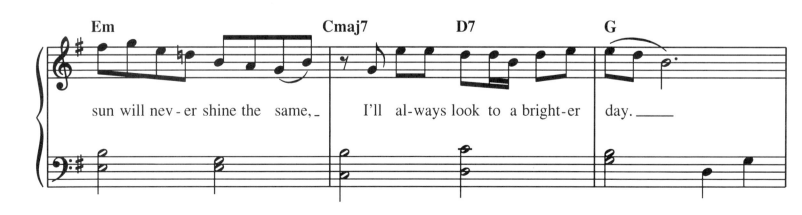

sun will nev - er shine the same, _ I'll al-ways look to a bright-er day. ____

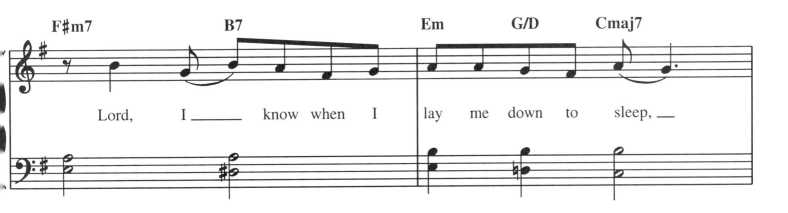

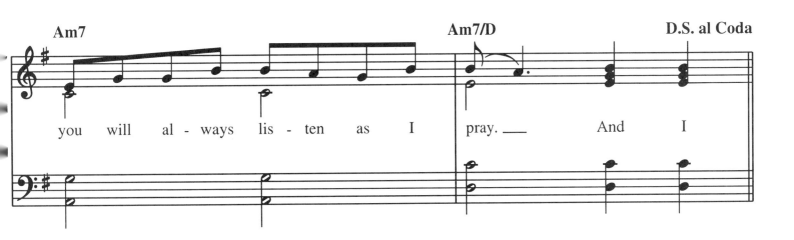

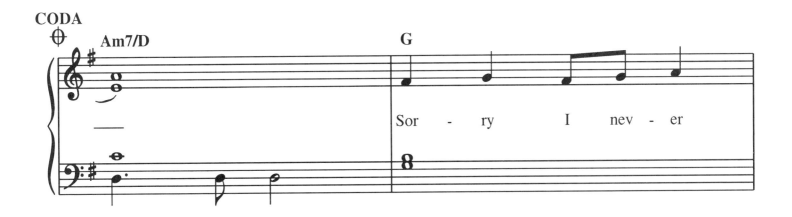

THE POWER OF LOVE

Words by MARY SUSAN APPLEGATE and JENNIFER RUSH
Music by CANDY DEROUGE and GUNTHER MENDE

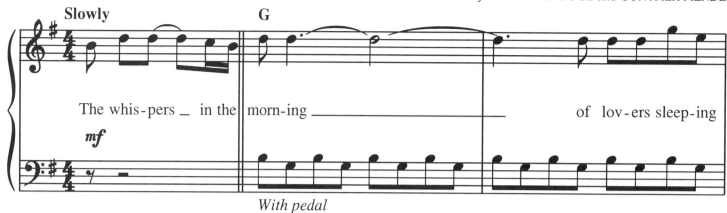

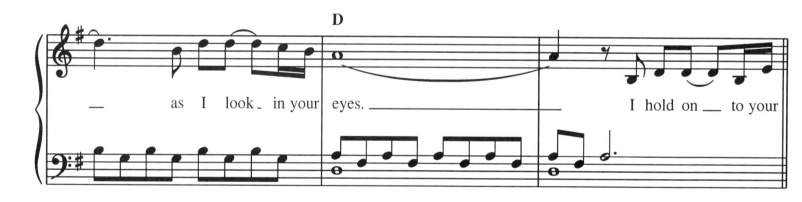

THE RIVER OF DREAMS

Words and Music by
BILLY JOEL

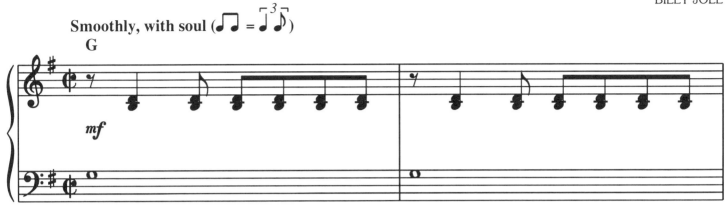

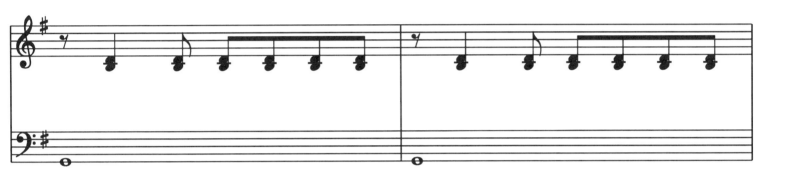

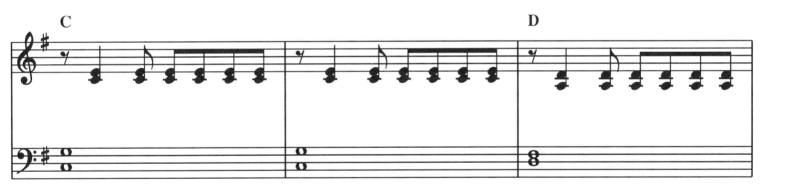

In the mid-dle of the night _____ I go walk-ing in my
night _____ I go walk-ing in my

172

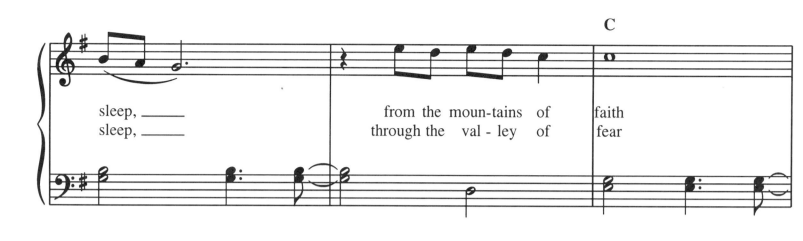

sleep, _____   from the moun-tains   of   faith
sleep, _____   through the   val - ley   of   fear

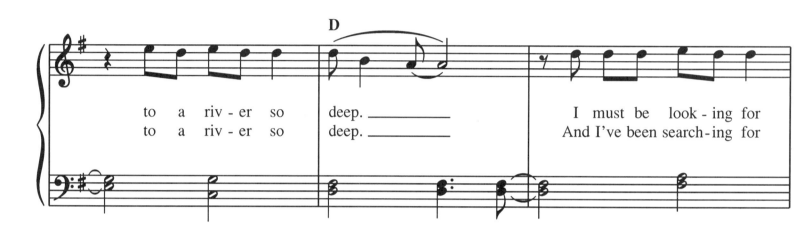

to   a   riv - er   so   deep. _____   I   must   be   look - ing   for
to   a   riv - er   so   deep. _____   And I've been search - ing   for

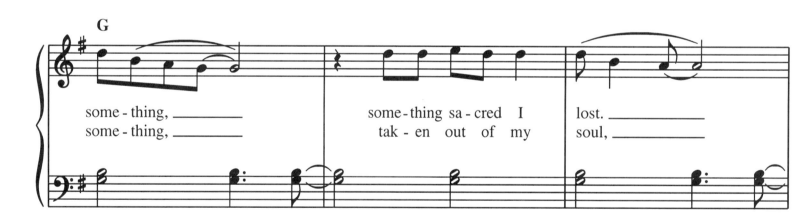

some - thing, _____   some - thing sa - cred   I   lost. _____
some - thing, _____   tak - en   out   of   my   soul, _____

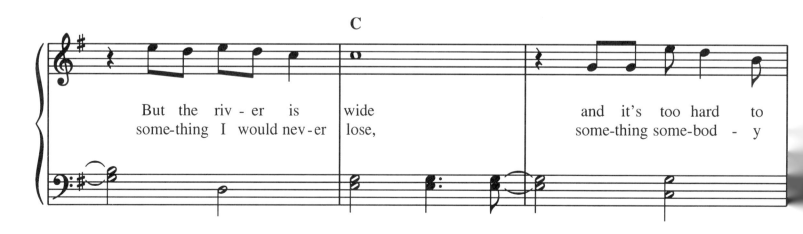

But   the   riv - er   is   wide   and   it's   too   hard   to
some - thing I   would   nev - er   lose,   some - thing   some - bod   -   y

In the mid-dle of the night, _____ I go walk-ing in my
night, _____ I go walk-ing in my

sleep, _____ through the jun - gle of doubt
sleep, _____ through the des - ert of truth

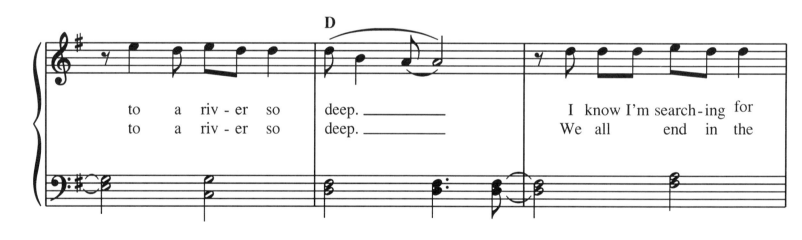

to a riv - er so deep. _____ I know I'm search-ing for
to a riv - er so deep. _____ We all end in the

some - thing, _____ some-thing so un - de - fined _____
o - cean, _____ we all start in the streams. _____

fire, I wade _ in-to the riv-er that runs _ to the prom-ised land. _

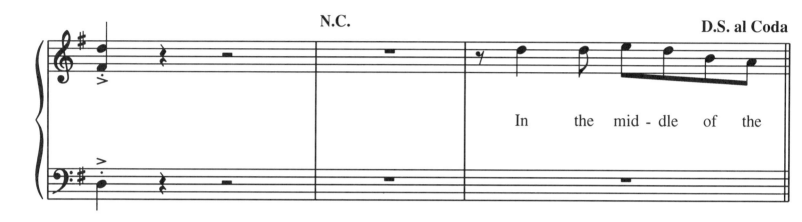

In the mid-dle of the

D.S. al Coda

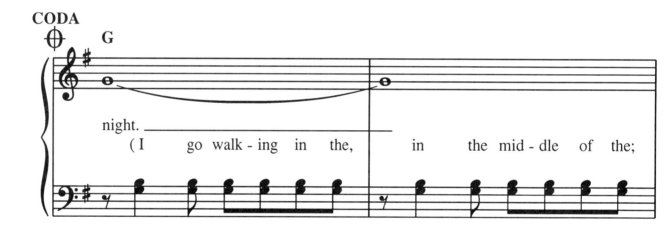

CODA **G**

night. _____
(I go walk-ing in the, in the mid-dle of the;

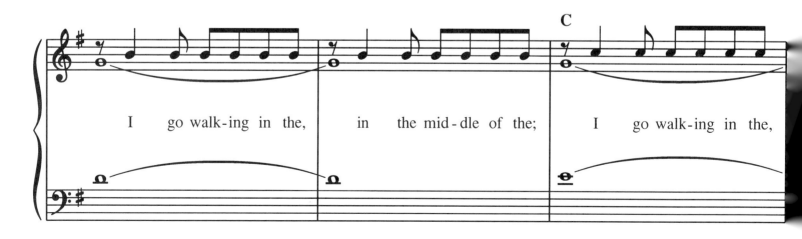

I go walk-ing in the, in the mid-dle of the; I go walk-ing in the,

in the mid - dle of the; I go walk-ing in the, in the mid - dle of the,

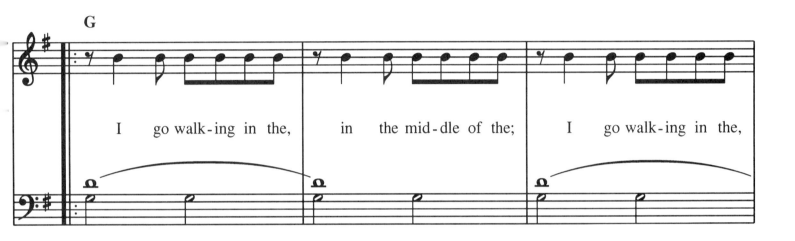

I go walk-ing in the, in the mid-dle of the; I go walk-ing in the,

in the mid - dle of the; I go walk-ing in the, in the mid-dle of the,

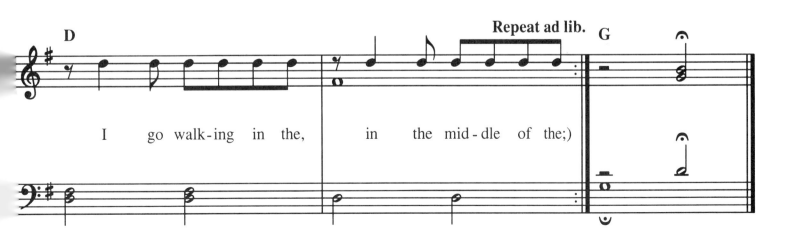

I go walk-ing in the, in the mid - dle of the;)

Repeat ad lib.

SAVE THE BEST FOR LAST

Words and Music by PHIL GALDSTON,
JON LIND and WENDY WALDMAN

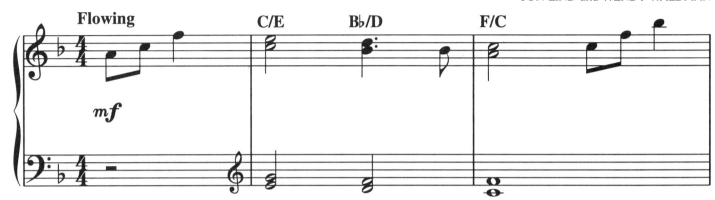

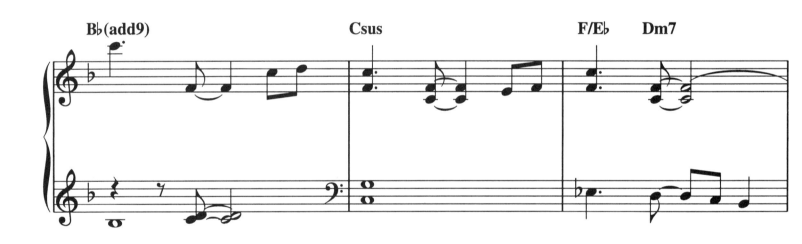

Some-times the snow comes down_ in June. Some-times the
nights you came_ to me when some sil - ly
snow comes down_ in June. Some-times the

sun goes 'round _ the moon. I see the pas - sion in _____ your
girl had set ___ you free. You won-dered how you'd make __ it
sun goes 'round _ the moon. Just when I thought a chance_ had

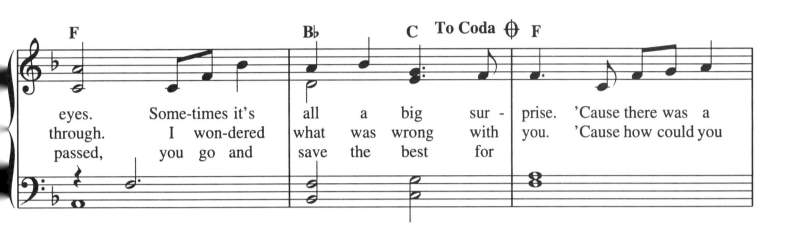

eyes. Some-times it's all a big sur - prise. 'Cause there was a
through. I won-dered what was wrong with you. 'Cause how could you
passed, you go and save the best for

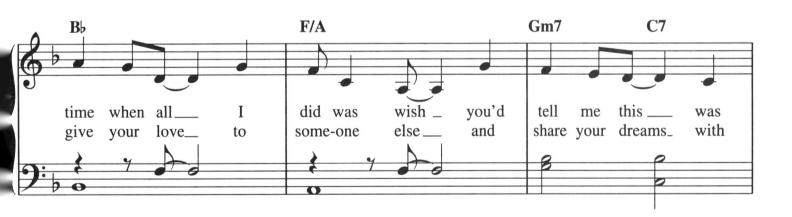

time when all___ I did was wish _ you'd tell me this ___ was
give your love_ to some-one else___ and share your dreams_ with

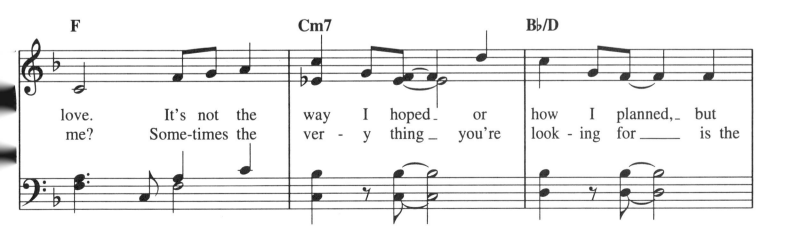

love. It's not the way I hoped_ or how I planned,_ but
me? Some-times the ver - y thing _ you're look - ing for _____ is the

some-how   it's   e - nough.   And   now   we're   stand - ing   face __   to
one   thing   you   can't   see.   But   now   we're   stand - ing   face __   to

face.
face.   }   Is - n't   this   world   a   cra - zy   place?   Just   when   I

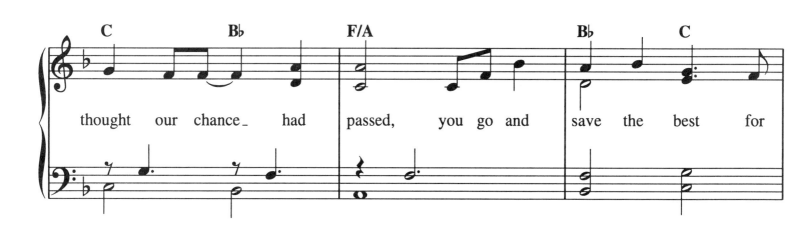

thought   our   chance __   had   passed,   you   go   and   save   the   best   for

last.

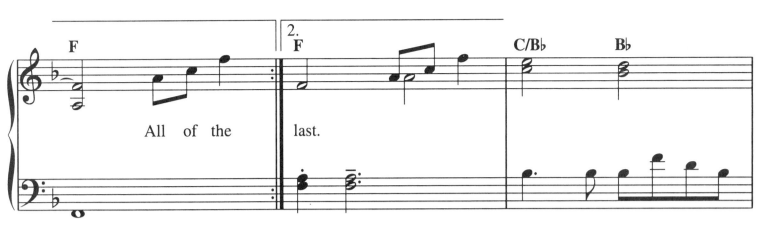

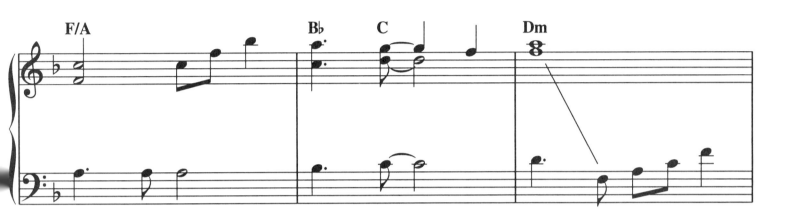

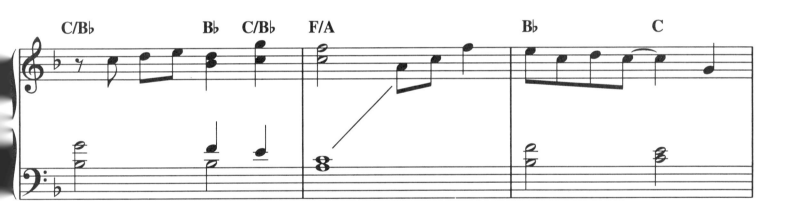

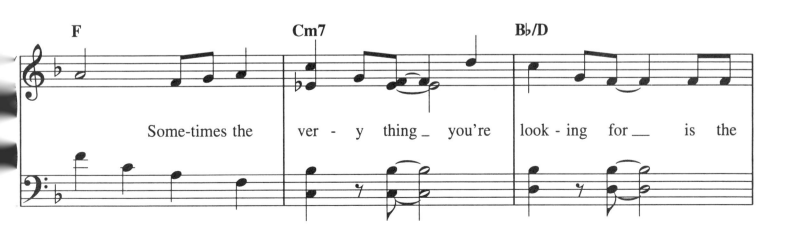

182

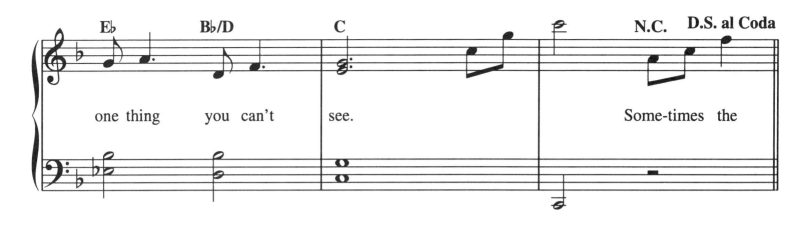

THE SIGN

Words and Music by buddha, joker,
jenny and linn

184

sign. No one's gon - na drag you up to get in - to the light where you ___ be - long ___

___ (But where do you be - long? ___)

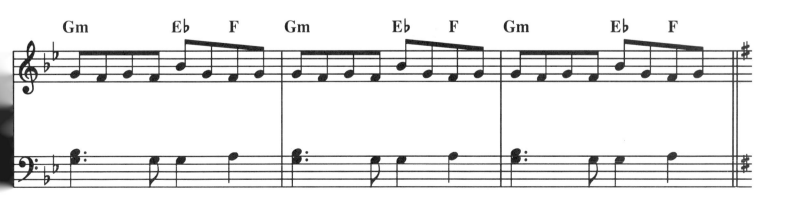

186

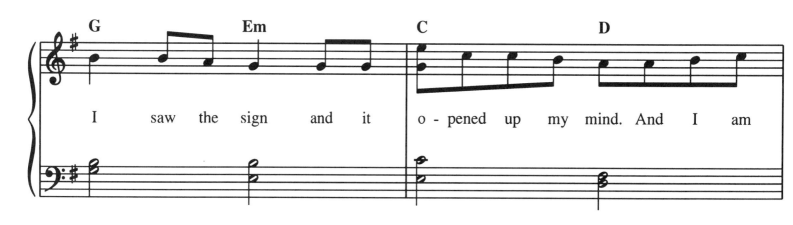

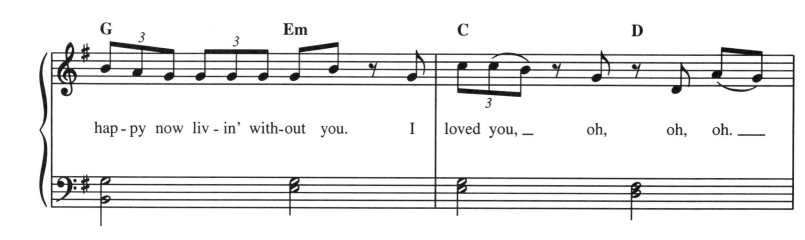

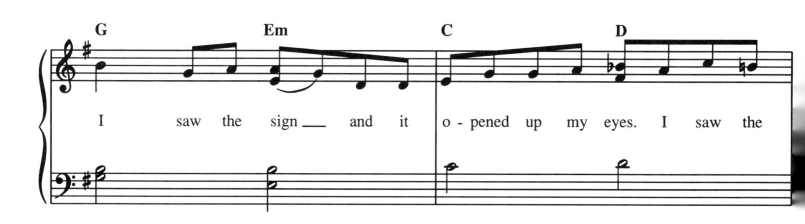

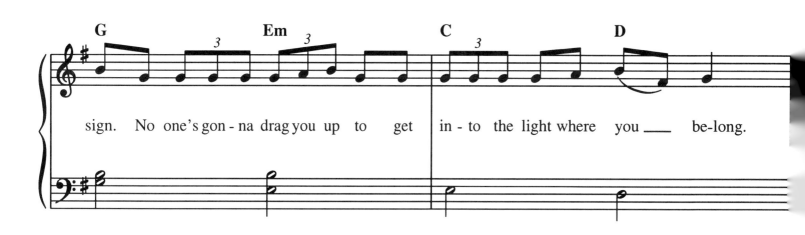

I saw the sign I saw the sign. _____ I saw the sign.

I saw the sign. I saw the sign. _____

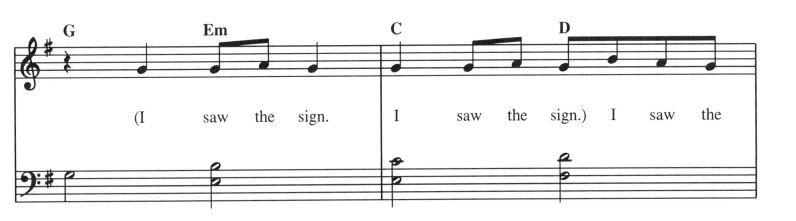

(I saw the sign. I saw the sign.) I saw the

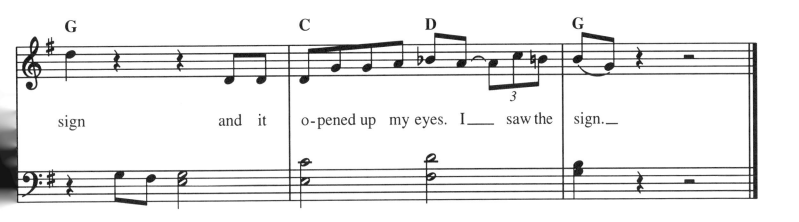

sign and it o-pened up my eyes. I___ saw the sign.__

THEME FROM "SCHINDLER'S LIST"

from the Universal Motion Picture SCHINDLER'S LIST

Composed by
JOHN WILLIAMS

MCA music publishing

TEARS IN HEAVEN

Words and Music by ERIC CLAPTON
and WILL JENNINGS

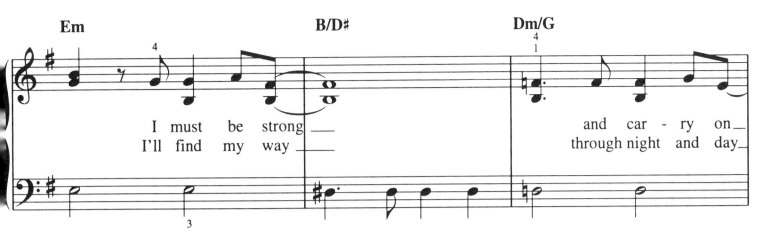

Em   B/D♯   Dm/G

I must be strong ___   and car - ry on___
I'll find my way ___   through night and day___

E   Am   D7sus   **To Coda**

___ 'cause I know ___   I don't be - long ___   here in heav -
___ 'cause I know ___   I just can't stay___   here in heav -

G   D/F♯   Em   G/D   1. C/E   D7sus   D7

en.
en.

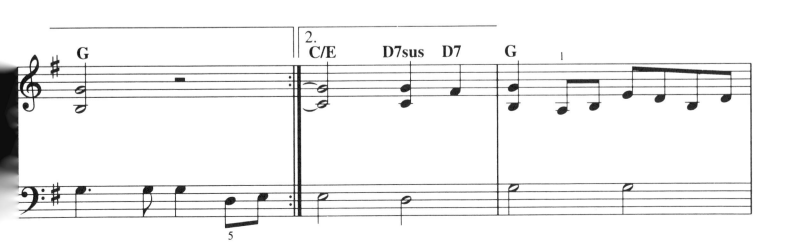

G   2. C/E   D7sus   D7   G

192

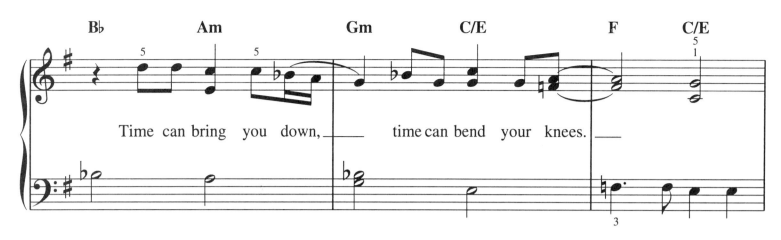

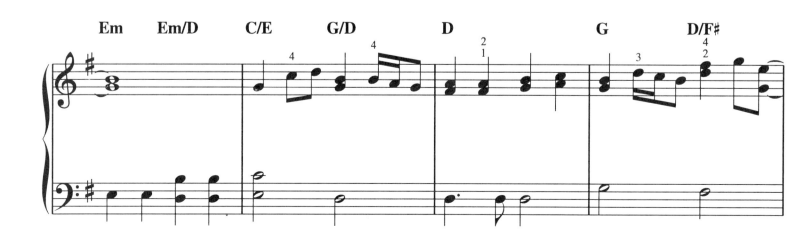

193

Be-yond the door

there's peace, I'm sure.___ And I know___

D.S. al Coda

___ there'll be no more ___ tears in heav - en.

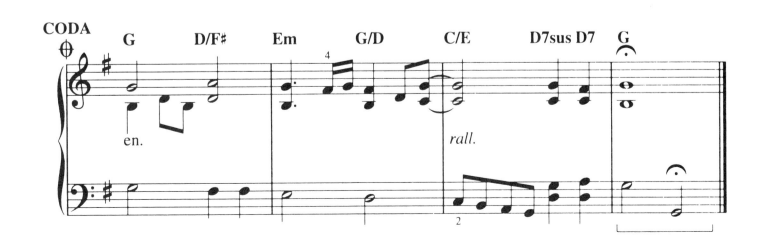

en. *rall.*

VISION OF LOVE

Words and Music by MARIAH CAREY
and BEN MARGULIES

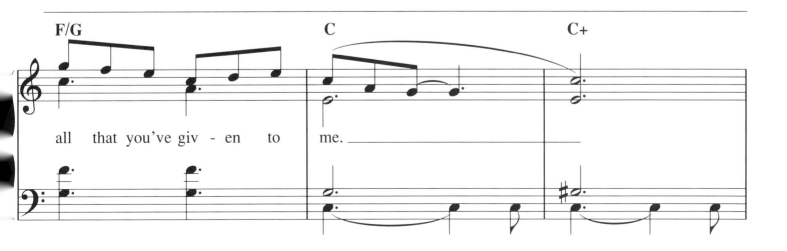

196

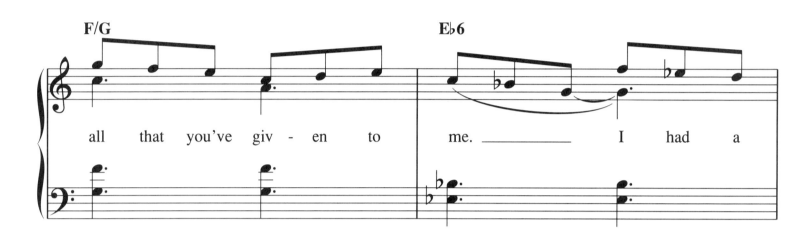

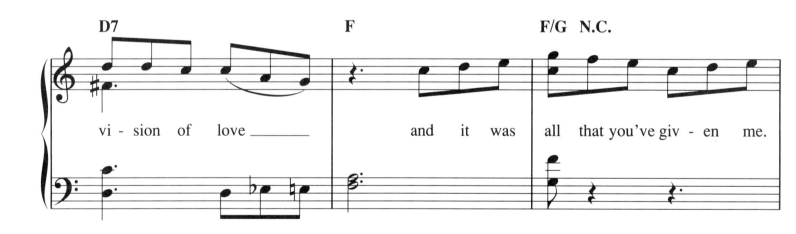

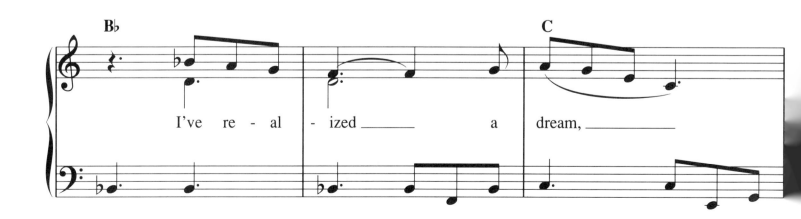

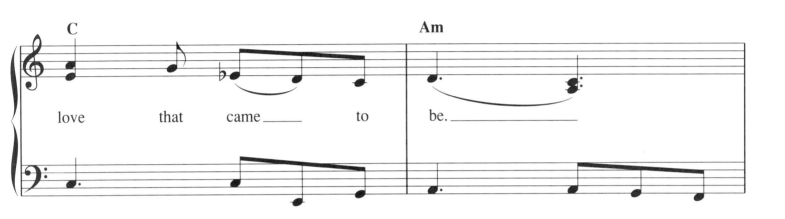

198

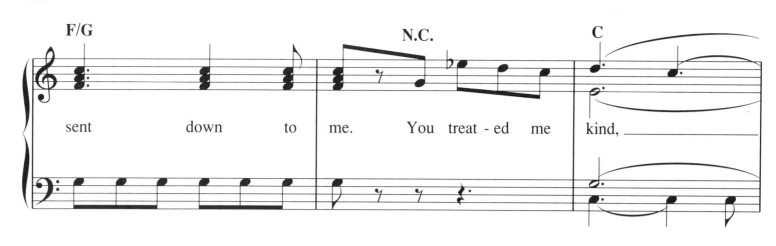

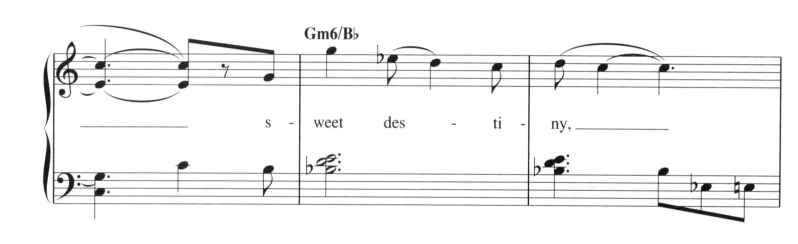

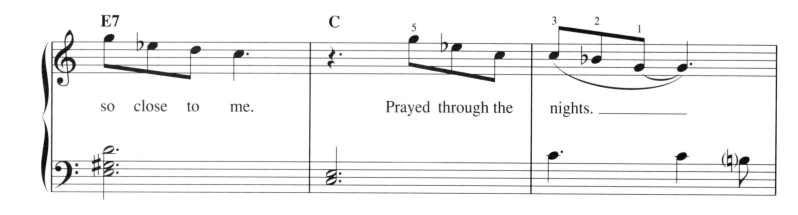

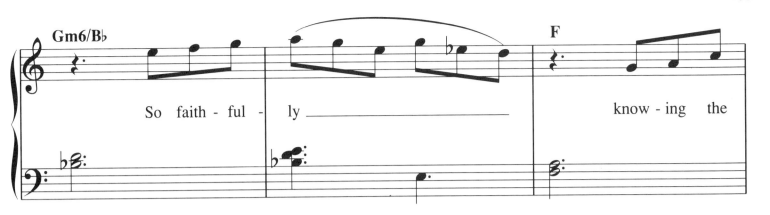

So faith-ful-ly _____ know-ing the

one that I need-ed would_ find me e-ven-tu-al-ly.

I had a vi-sion of love _____ and it was

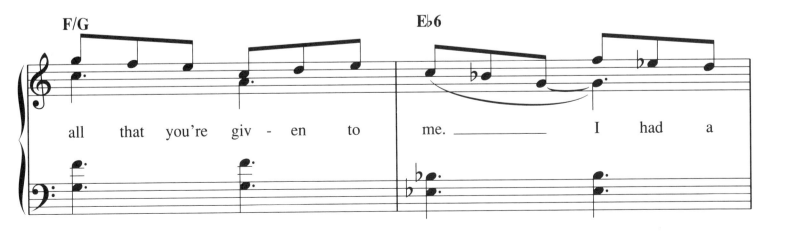

all that you're giv-en to me. _____ I had a

WHEN I FALL IN LOVE

Words by EDWARD HEYMAN
Music by VICTOR YOUNG

rest - less world like this is, _____ love is end - ed be - fore it's be -

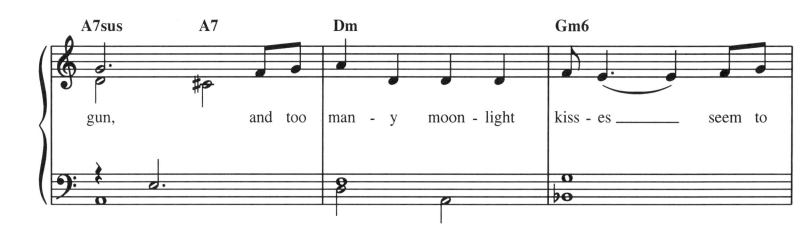

gun, and too man - y moon - light kiss - es _____ seem to

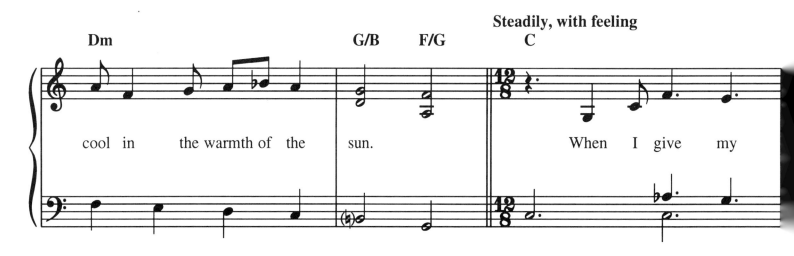

cool in the warmth of the sun. When I give my

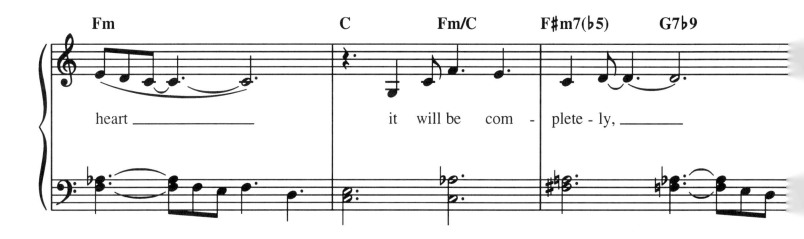

heart _____ it will be com - plete - ly, _____

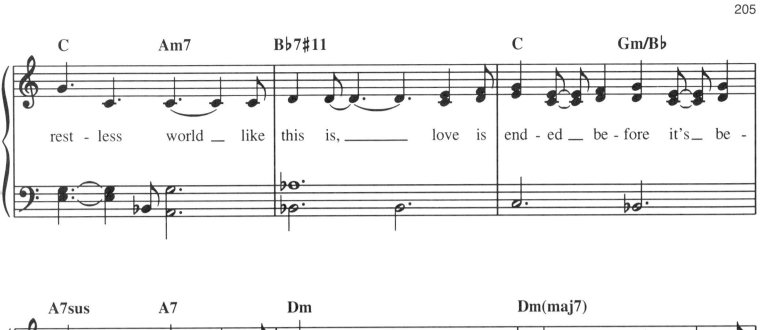

rest - less world __ like this is, _____ love is end - ed __ be - fore it's __ be -

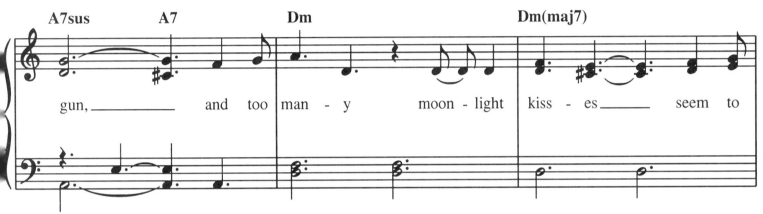

gun, _____ and too man - y moon - light kiss - es _____ seem to

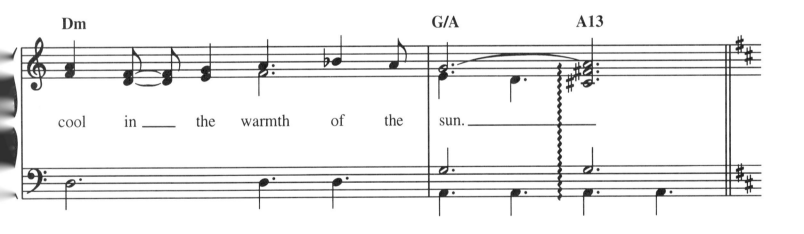

cool in ___ the warmth of the sun. _____

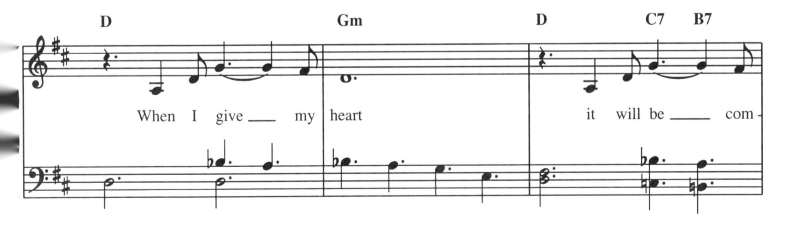

When I give ___ my heart it will be ___ com -

206

207

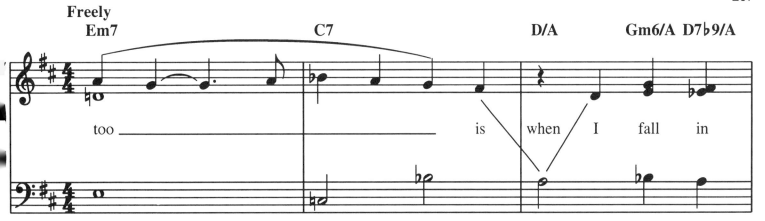

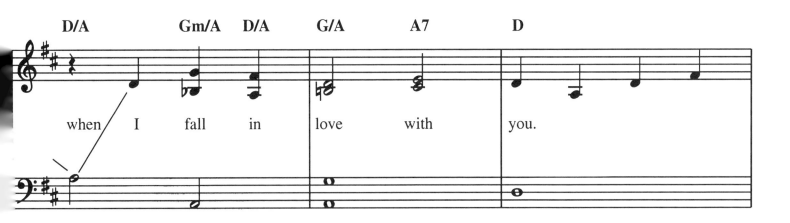

WITH ONE LOOK

from SUNSET BOULEVARD

Music by ANDREW LLOYD WEBBER
Lyrics by DON BLACK and CHRISTOPHER HAMPTON,
with contributions by AMY POWERS

Slowly

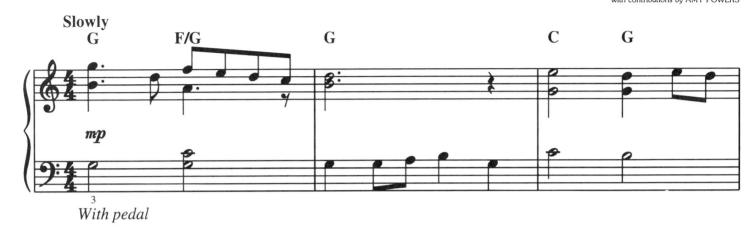

NORMA: With one look I can break your heart,

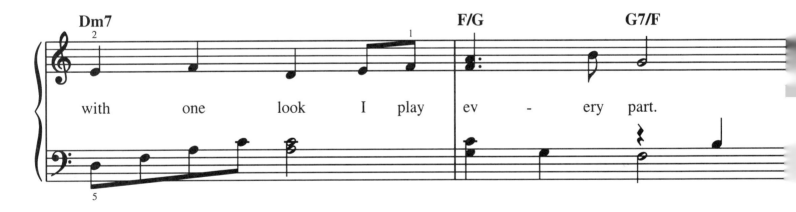

with one look I play ev - ery part.

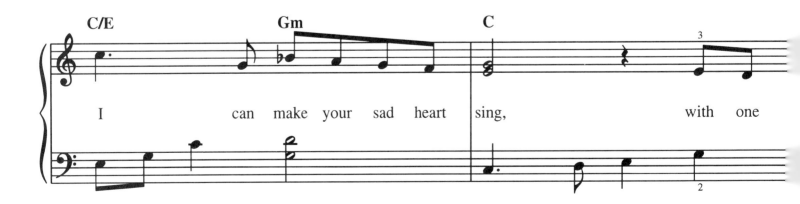

I can make your sad heart sing, with one

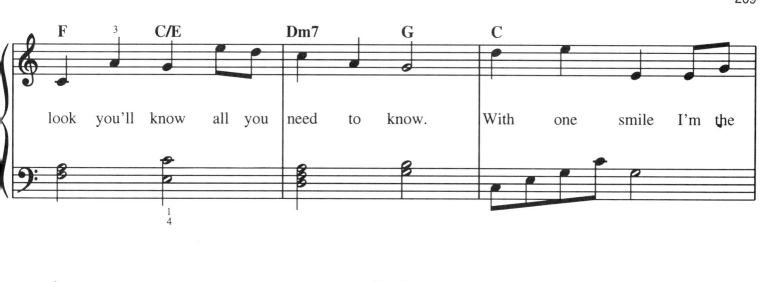

look you'll know all you need to know. With one smile I'm the

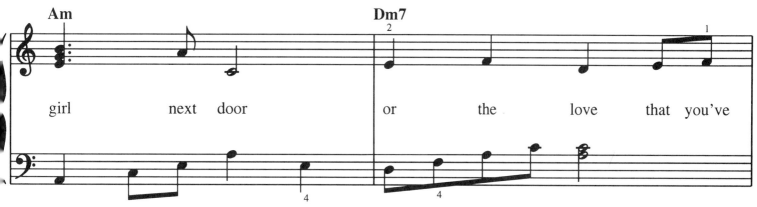

girl next door or the love that you've

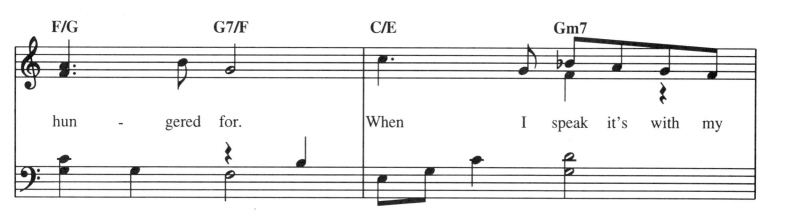

hun - gered for. When I speak it's with my

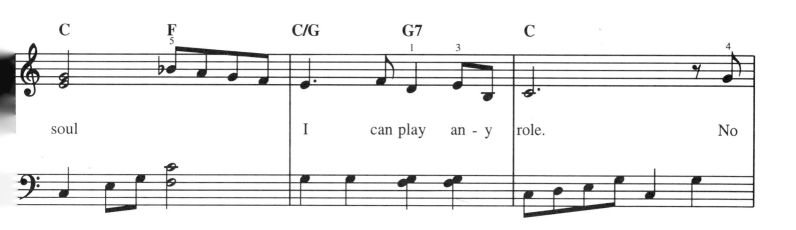

soul I can play an - y role. No

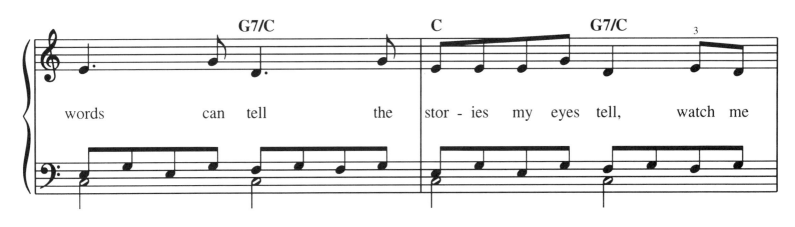

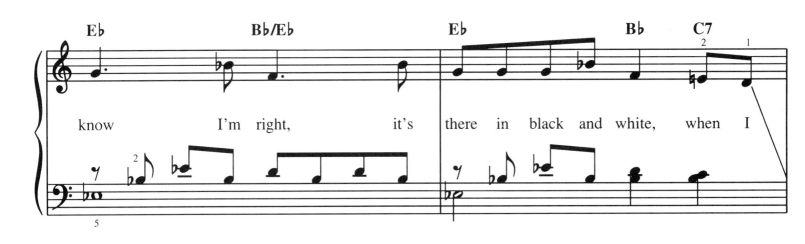

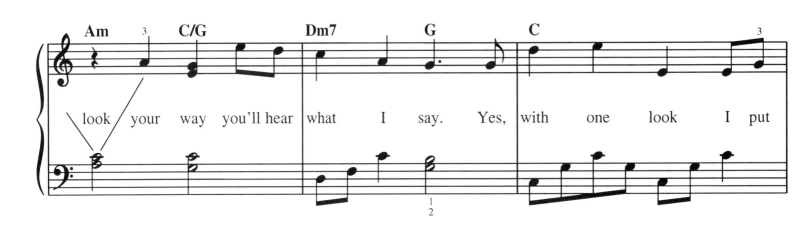

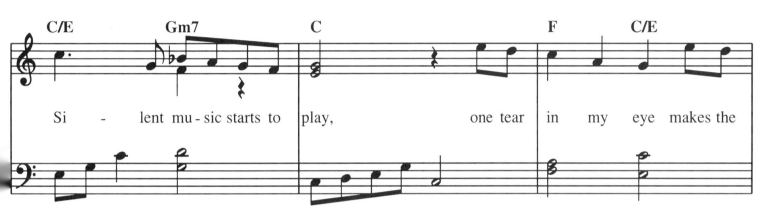

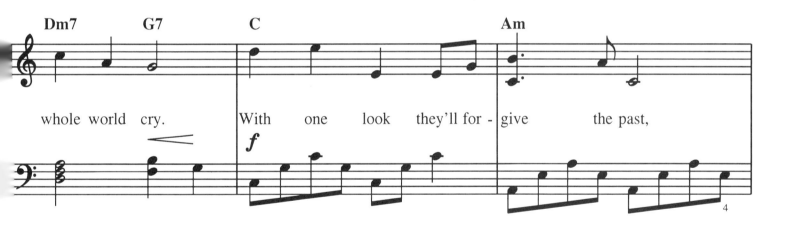

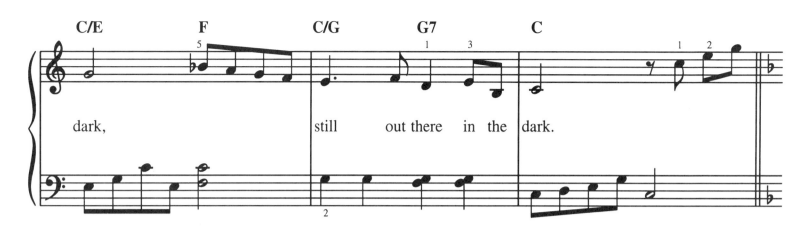

dark, still out there in the dark.

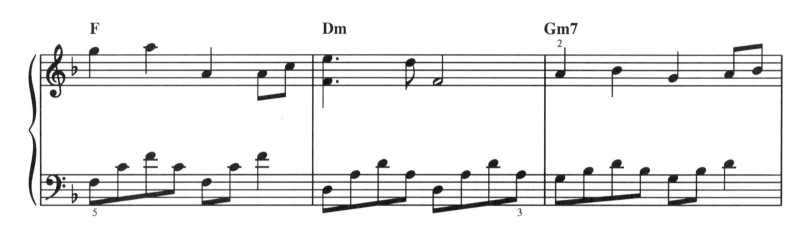

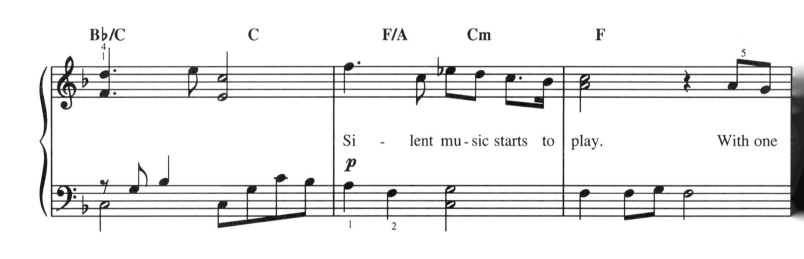

Si - lent mu-sic starts to play. With one

look you'll know all you need to know. With one look I'll ig-

A WHOLE NEW WORLD
(Aladdin's Theme)
from Walt Disney's ALADDIN

Music by ALAN MENKEN
Lyrics by TIM RICE

Slowly and sweetly

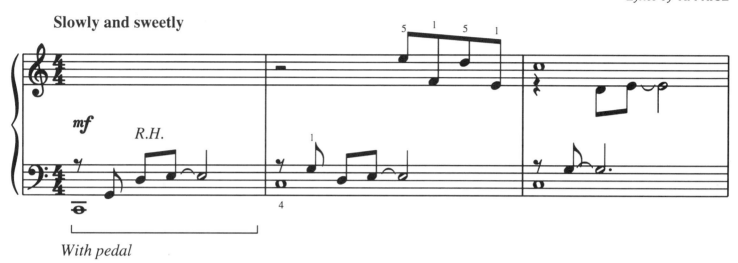

With pedal

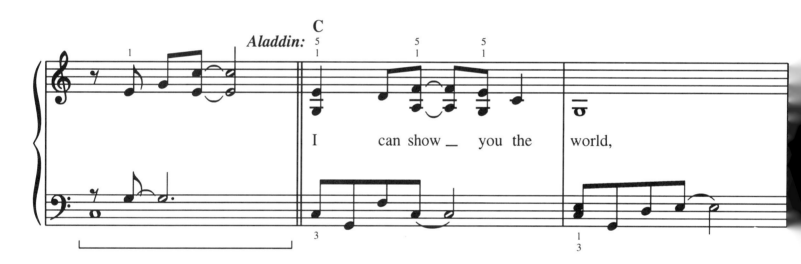

Aladdin: I can show you the world,

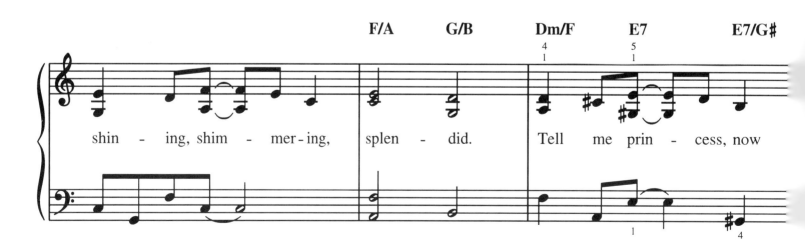

shin - ing, shim - mer-ing, splen - did. Tell me prin - cess, now

when did you last let your heart __ de - cide?

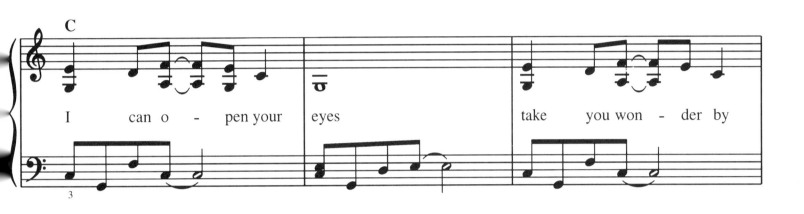

I can o - pen your eyes take you won - der by

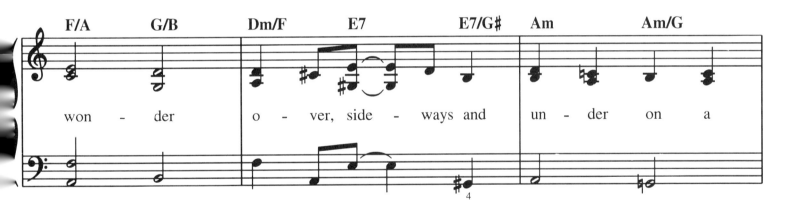

won - der o - ver, side - ways and un - der on a

mag-ic car - pet ride. A whole new world

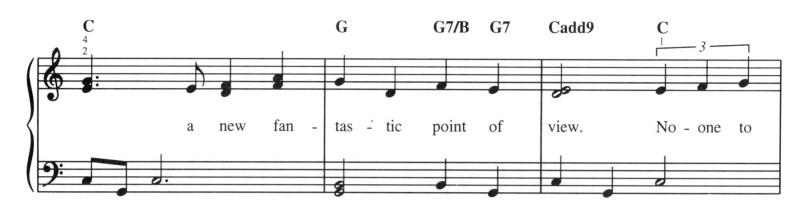

a new fan - tas - tic point of view. No - one to

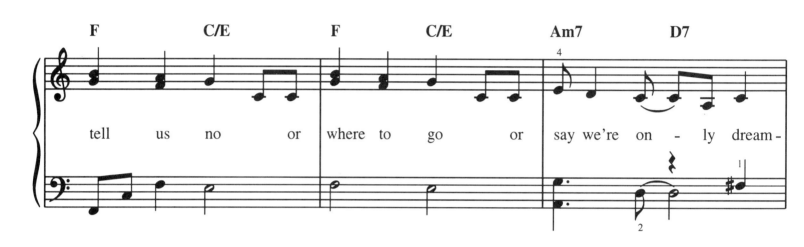

tell us no or where to go or say we're on - ly dream-

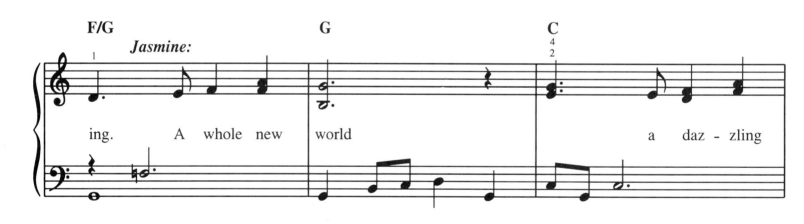

Jasmine:

ing. A whole new world a daz - zling

place I nev - er knew. But when I'm way up here it's

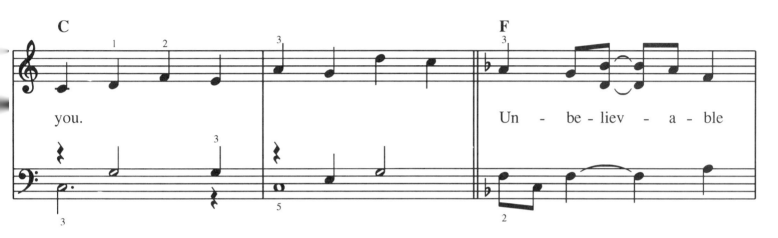

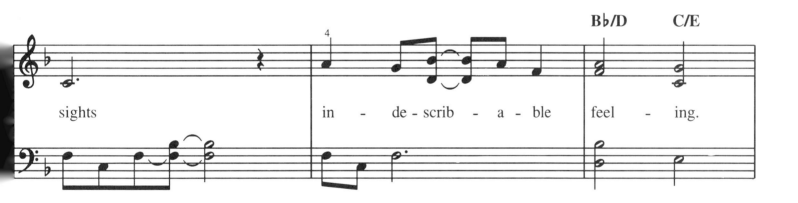

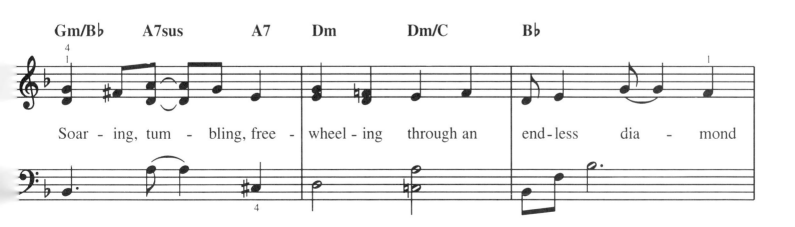

sky.   A   whole new   world   a   hun - dred

thou - sand   things   to   see.   I'm   like   a

shoot - ing   star.   I've   come   so   far   I

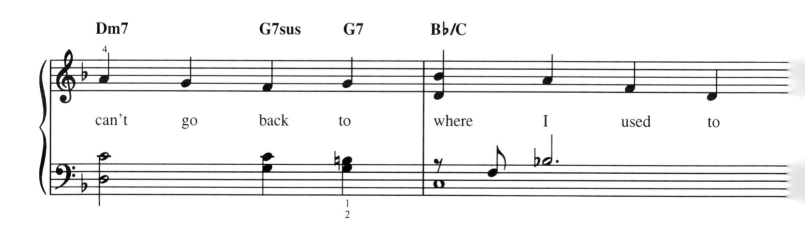

can't   go   back   to   where   I   used   to

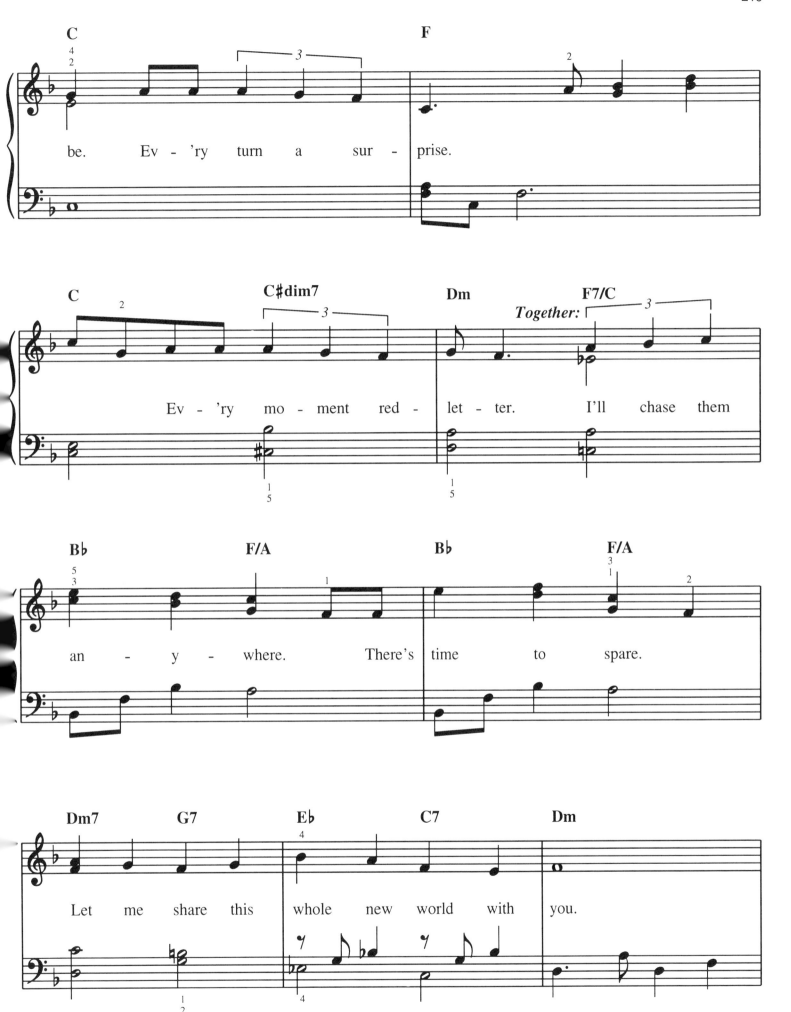

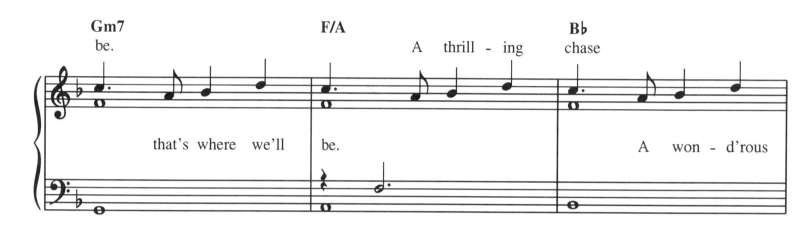

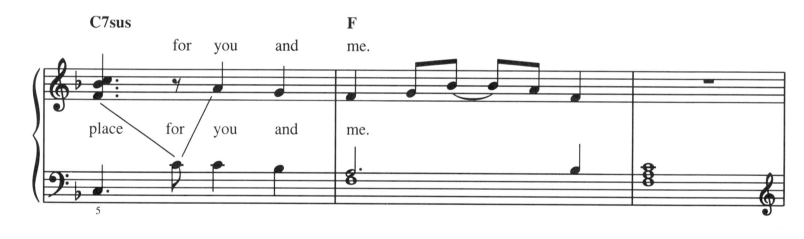

YOU MUST LOVE ME
from the Cinergi Motion Picture EVITA

Lyric by TIM RICE
Music by ANDREW LLOYD WEBBER

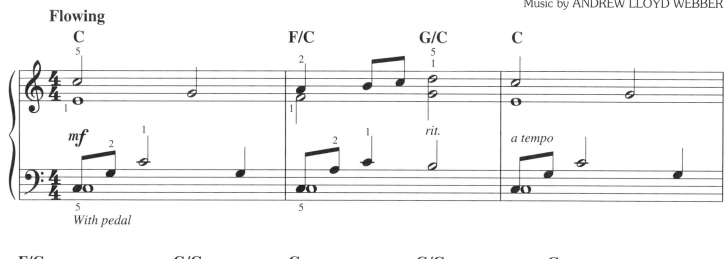

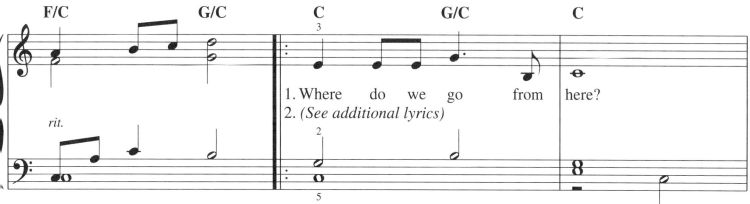

1. Where do we go from here?
2. (See additional lyrics)

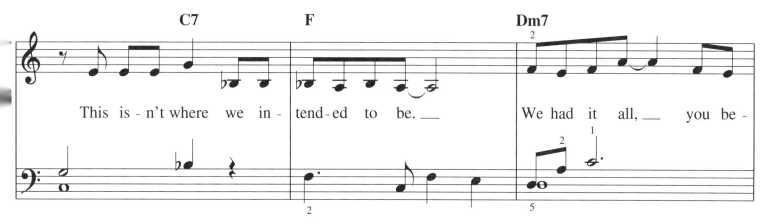

This is-n't where we in-tend-ed to be. ___ We had it all, ___ you be-

lieved _ in me, ___ I be- lieved _ in you. _

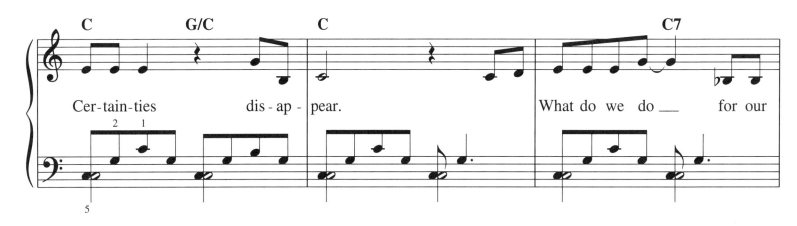

Cer-tain-ties dis-ap-pear. What do we do ___ for our

dream to sur-vive, how do we keep ___ all our pas-sions a-live as

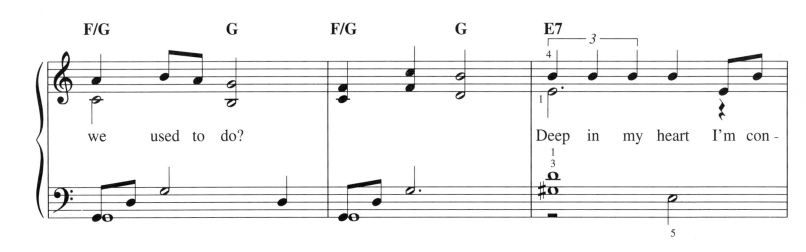

we used to do? Deep in my heart I'm con-

ceal-ing things that I'm long-ing to say,